CAMBRIDGE PRIMARY
Science

Teacher's Resource

2

Jon Board and Alan Cross

CAMBRIDGE
UNIVERSITY PRESS

CAMBRIDGE
UNIVERSITY PRESS

University Printing House, Cambridge CB2 8BS, United Kingdom

Cambridge University Press is part of the University of Cambridge.

It furthers the University's mission by disseminating knowledge in the pursuit of education, learning and research at the highest international levels of excellence.

Information on this title: education.cambridge.org

© Cambridge University Press 2014

First published 2014
3rd printing 2015

Printed in the United Kingdom by Printondemand-worldwide, Peterborough

A catalogue record for this publication is available from the British Library

ISBN 978-1107-61148-1 Paperback

Cover artwork: Bill Bolton

....

The publisher is grateful to the experienced teachers Mansoora Shoaib Shah, Lahore Grammar School, 55 Main, Gulberg, Lahore and Lynne Ransford for their careful reviewing of the content.

Contents

Contents

Introduction

The *Cambridge Primary Science* series has been developed to match the Cambridge International Examinations Primary Science curriculum framework. It is a fun, flexible and easy-to-use course that gives both learners and teachers the support they need. In keeping with the aims of the curriculum itself, it encourages learners to be actively engaged with the content and to develop enquiry skills as well as subject knowledge.

This Teacher's Resource for Stage 2 gives extensive support for teaching Stage 2 of the curriculum framework. It frequently references the *Learner's Book*, ISBN 978-1-107-61139-9 and *Activity Book*, ISBN 978-1-107-61143-6, for Stage 2, offering guidance on how to get the best out of using those products. There are also many additional teaching ideas for you to choose from.

The main sections in this *Teacher's Resource* are:

Teaching ideas. These give you a whole range of ideas on how to present the topics in the classroom. This includes ideas for classroom activities, assessment and differentiation, and suggestions for ICT resources. References to the *Learner's Book* and *Activity Book* are provided throughout, including guidance notes on the activities suggested in the *Learner's Book*. The teaching ideas are also available in editable format on the CD-ROM included with this Teacher's Resource, so that you can include your own notes.

Worksheets. A large collection of worksheets offers further activity and exercise ideas, in addition to those included in the *Learner's Book* and *Activity Book*, while other worksheets are intended to support the *Learner's Book* activities. The worksheets are also available in editable format on the CD-ROM included with this *Teacher's Resource*, so that you can adapt them to your own needs.

Pictures. A selection of high-resolution pictures has been provided on the CD-ROM for use on an interactive whiteboard, or for learners to view on digital devices at school if you have that facility. You might also print the pictures out for learners to look at. Suggestions on how to use these pictures to consolidate and extend learning are provided in the teaching ideas.

Answers to questions. Answers to all the questions from the *Learner's Book*, the exercises in the *Activity Book* and the worksheets in this resource are provided.

We hope you enjoy using this series.

With best wishes,
the Cambridge Primary Science team.

Teaching sequence

Throughout the *Cambridge Primary Science* series, the units are presented in the same order as in the Cambridge International Examinations Primary Science curriculum framework, for easy navigation and to help you ensure that the curriculum is covered. However, this is not necessarily the best sequence in which to teach the material. For example, all the biology topics would be taught in one large block, whereas you may prefer to present a more balanced and varied route through the different areas of science.

When planning your teaching sequence, it is advisable to think about how the science topics fit in with the other subjects you teach. You should also consider topics within the science curriculum that are best taught at a particular time of year. For example, Unit 1 Going outside is best taught in the warmer months when learners can observe plants and animals. This will depend on the local climate.

Unit 3 Changing materials includes lots of hands-on testing for learners. It might therefore be a useful unit to teach early on so as to establish the importance of learner independence in investigations. Unit 4 Light and dark is best taught before Unit 6 The Earth and the Sun which may require a clearer understanding of light and dark; but this is by no means essential. If you are in a part of the world that experiences clear seasons, it would be better to teach Unit 4 at a time of year when it is likely to be sunny, and the days are not too short. This way you can make the most of the opportunity to examine shadows outside.

Learners might see these six topics at Stage 2 as quite separate. You should point clearly to links between the content of the different units. For example, Units 2 and 3 both examine the different properties of various materials, which builds on knowledge from Stage 1. Further links that can be made are suggested in the Teaching ideas.

These are two alternative sequences you might consider, though you may invent your own. Biology units are dark grey, chemistry units light grey and physics units white.

Sequence 1:

Unit 1 Going outside	Unit 3 Changing materials	Unit 2 Looking at rocks	Unit 5 Electricity	Unit 4 Light and dark	Unit 6 The Earth and the Sun

Sequence 2:

Unit 3 Changing materials	Unit 5 Electricity	Unit 4 Light and dark	Unit 6 The Earth and the Sun	Unit 2 Looking at rocks	Unit 1 Going outside

Scientific enquiry

Scientific enquiry is about how scientific ideas emerge, supported by investigations and evaluating the data and other evidence that are produced through those investigations. The ideas underpin all areas of science. Therefore, the scientific enquiry section of the curriculum framework is not included as a separate teaching unit in the teaching sequences suggested above. Rather, scientific enquiry should be taught in an integrated fashion, alongside teaching of the other content areas.

The *Cambridge Primary Science* series has been written to support this way of working. By allowing learners to carry out the activities in the Learner's Book you will cover all the scientific enquiry objectives in the curriculum framework. These activities can be supported by further activities suggested in the teaching ideas and worksheets in this Teacher's Resource, and through the exercises focused on planning investigations and evaluating data in the Activity Book.

Here, we give a further introduction to the scientific enquiry objectives listed in the Cambridge Primary Science curriculum framework for Stage 2. For each framework statement, some background information is given on the level that learners are expected to achieve at this stage. Also, some specific examples are given of activities suggested in this series that can be used to help learners develop each skill.

Ideas and evidence

Collect evidence by making observations when trying to answer a science question.
Learners may collect evidence in the form of pictures, numbers and words through hands-on investigations and research in age-appropriate books. Teachers should model these skills and organise opportunities for shared writing and discussion of evidence. Encourage learners to have a science question in mind as they collect evidence, and to find evidence that will help to answer that specific question. It will help them to work sometimes in pairs and groups and sometimes alone. They should gather information from a range of sources and by counting and measuring using standard and non-standard measures. The skill of collecting evidence should be developed across the whole stage, but examples could include: Learner's Book Activity 1.3 Today's weather; Worksheet 2.3c How good is soil for growing seeds?

Use first-hand experience, e.g. observe melting ice.
Learners should be given every opportunity to learn from observation of first-hand experience. Try to ensure that all learners (or as many as possible) are able to handle and describe materials and experiences. They should use their senses of sight, touch and hearing. Encourage them to discuss what they experience and whether it reinforces previous similar experiences or is different in some way. Ensure that you model careful observation and, importantly, the correct science vocabulary relevant to the experience. The key word in this objective is 'use', so bear in mind that learners should not just have experiences, but also use those experiences to further their learning. Observations can be used to identify similarity and difference, use vocabulary, elicit understanding, generate questions and record observations in many different forms. You may have to model the use of first-hand experiences, for example by pointing out similarities as well as differences. The materials provide numerous opportunities including: Learner's Book Activity 2.3 Finding the rock in soil; Activity Book Exercise 1.3 Our weather.

Introduction

Use simple information sources.
A range of simple information sources should be used by learners. These will include the results of their observations and investigations, and suitable secondary sources such as internet sites and books. Again learners need to use the information, which means more than just gather it. They can use it to check out ideas they may have, to answer questions, to extend the range of information available, to generate more questions, to look for patterns, to identify examples and to define ideas. Examples of such information sources include websites such as www.bbc.co.uk/learningzone/clips/how-have-different-animals-adapted-to-their-habitats/12665.html, which shows a four-minute clip of animals in hot, cold, wet and dry environments. Many more websites are suggested throughout the Teaching ideas.

Plan investigative work

Ask questions and suggest ways to answer them.
By encouraging your learners to ask science questions you are setting an excellent tone for your science teaching. Learners may need support framing questions in a scientific way, but they will be highly motivated by questions they generate themselves. Model and teach them question formats including: How far…? How many…? How fast…? Which is louder? Will it grow? Will it die? and What will happen if…? You should increasingly ask them to pose 'why' questions so that they are forced to consider explanations. Use numerous simple examples to model this process, such as Why do adult birds have babies? or Why do insects keep moving as if they are searching for something?

Predict what will happen before deciding what to do.
Make it routine that before a test, experiment or demonstration you ask the learners to say what they think will happen. Encourage them to explain how they arrived at their prediction. This will be a challenge for some learners so they may need some support at this stage. The prediction can be given in any form. Do give attention and value to all predictions, emphasising that predictions do not have to be correct. What is important is that the prediction can be tested, and that the test will show whether or not the prediction was correct – either way, we have learnt something! Learners should then use their prediction to help them decide how they will carry out the test or experiment.

Recognise that a test or comparison may be unfair.
This is an important step towards being able to design a fair test. Allow the learners to consider and review potential investigations and discuss whether they are fair or not. You might initiate this with examples which are grossly unfair. It will assist some learners to see a potential test trialled so that they can see the element which is not fair. For example, you could demonstrate a test in which you compare how high two balls bounce, but drop the balls from different heights.

Obtain and present evidence

Make suggestions for collecting evidence.
Ensure that pairs and groups have time to consider how a test or investigation is carried out. This will give learners the opportunity to think about evidence they might collect. It will help them if they understand the science question being addressed and then consider variables which they might change, measure/observe or control. Do give time to all suggestions as you want to encourage everyone to contribute. Learners may make suggestions which are not used but these are still acceptable suggestions. Opportunities for developing this skill can be found throughout the materials; for example, in Activity 1.1 Compare two different places learners can suggest which two different places they want to investigate.

Talk about risks and how to avoid danger.
It is worthwhile to shift a little responsibility onto the learners by asking them to think about risks posed to themselves and others by their investigation. A few minutes spent as a pair, group or class considering potential risks will result in a safer classroom and also in learners increasingly thinking about harmful consequences. Challenge them to suggest ways to make the activities as safe as possible. Ultimately, it is of course your responsibility to ensure that activities are safe. But, involving the learners is one very effective way of making sure they understand ideas about safety. Unit 3 has many opportunities to think about risk in the activities that involve heating different materials.

Make and record observations.
Learners should make a variety of different observations, which they then record. These include drawings and sketches, photographs and writing. They should use different senses and realise that this is an important part of what scientists do. Learners should use their observations to confirm or reject predictions, to make comparisons and to identify similarity and difference. Making and recording observations should be a key part of any activity. But you can particularly focus on this skill in Unit 1 where learners are expected to make observations of the weather and record data.

Take simple measurements.
Many of the materials provided cater for measurements in non-standard units. For example, Exercise 6.3 in the Activity Book asks learners to measure the length of shadows using counters or coins. As you progress through the mathematics curriculum, you can also allow learners to make measurements of length and time in standard units in a science context. Indeed, this is a good way of reinforcing the skills learnt in mathematics. Other phenomena may be measured more qualitatively, and may be based on comparison. For example, in Worksheet 1.3d learners make a wind meter and use this to make qualitative measurements of the wind strength. Measurements on different days can then be compared.

Use a variety of ways to tell others what happened.
In the future, learners should be able to select the means by which they will describe their findings. At this stage, you should create opportunities to try out a range of methods and consider how effective they are. These might include forms of writing, drawings, sketches, models, audio recording, photographs and film. You can create these opportunities for any activities, but learners can be particularly creative in sharing their weather observations in Unit 1, and their observations of shadows in Units 4 and 6.

Consider evidence and approach

Make comparisons.
Learners should make comparisons in observations and in results from their investigations. They should seek similarities and differences and examples they find unexpected. These are often examples which allow learners to review their understanding. The materials include many opportunities for comparisons. Sometimes these are obvious, such as in Activity 1.1 where learners compare the living organisms they find in two different places. However, learners should also begin to realise that they are making comparisons in other situations, and that conclusions can be drawn from the comparisons. For example, in Activity 4.1 they are comparing how different objects appear in a dark place, from which they can conclude that some of these objects are light sources while others are not.

Introduction

Identify simple patterns and associations.
Learners should consider observations and evidence carefully to establish any patterns. This may help learners to spot that one thing leads to another, or that two phenomena always appear together, which helps them to understand the science. This skill can be practised in many different contexts. For example, from the activities in Topic 5.4 learners should realise that there is a pattern in how the coloured wires from a buzzer or motor need to be connected to a cell to make a circuit work. Learners can use the patterns they identify to make further predictions. For example, learners can use the weather data they record in Unit 1 to see if they can predict the weather to come.

Talk about predictions (orally and in text), the outcome and why this happened.
Having made predictions in many activities in the materials, time should be found for learners to discuss and consider whether their observations support the different predictions made or not. They should look at different outcomes of activities and say why they think these things happened. Opportunities can be found in all the topics. Good examples include: Activity 3.4, where learners can discuss whether the effects of heating different foods were what they expected; Activity 4.4a, where learners study whether they can successfully make the hand shadows, and if not, what they are doing wrong.

Review and explain what happened.
This can be the most challenging part of science for younger children. However, this means that they can learn most from it. Some learners will need to talk about the investigations and review their results carefully. For example, after completing an investigation, ask learners to review the initial questions and determine the extent of their success in answering the question. They should also review their predictions, and determine whether or not the predictions were correct.. They may need to have time to talk about things that went well, difficulties they encountered, and things that surprised them. There are very good opportunities to practise this skill: for example, in Topic 3.3, both in Activity 3.3 where learners stretch elastic bands of different thicknesses, and in Worksheet 3.3d where learners stretch different materials. These activities lend themselves to thinking about scientific explanations for the observations recorded, as well as factors relating to the test itself such as whether it was fair, or would have been easier to do a different way.

The following table gives an overview of which resources are available in the Stage 2 products in this series to support each scientific enquiry objective.

Framework statement	Learner's Book	Activity Book	Teacher's Resource
Ideas and evidence			
Collect evidence by making observations when trying to answer a science question.	Activities 1.1, 1.2, 1.3, 2.1, 3.1, 3.3, 3.4, 4.1, 4.2, 5.1, 5.4a, 5.4b, 6.2, 6.3a, 6.3b	Exercise 1.3	Worksheets 1.3a, 1.3d, 2.1a, 2.1b, 2.3c, 2.3d, 3.1a, 3.3b, 3.3d, 3.4a, 3.4c, 3.5d, 4.2, 5.3b, 6.2a, 6.3
Use first-hand experience, e.g. observe melting ice.	Activities 1.1, 1.2, 1.3, 2.1, 2.2, 2.3, 2.4, 3.1, 3.2, 3.3, 3.4, 3.5, 4.1, 4.2, 4.3, 4.4a, 4.4b, 5.1, 5.3, 5.5, 6.2, 6.3a, 6.3b	Exercise 1.3	Worksheets 1.3a, 1.3d, 2.1a, 2.1b, 2.1c, 2.2b, 2.3a, 2.3b, 2.3c, 2.3d, 2.4a, 2.4b, 3.1, 3.2a, 3.2b, 3.3a, 3.3b, 3.3d, 3.4b, 3.4c, 3.5a, 3.5b, 3.5c, 3.5d, 4.1a, 4.2, 4.3a, 4.3b, 5.3b, 6.2a, 6.3
Use simple information sources.	Activities 1.4, 3.2, 3.4, 4.4a, 5.1, 5.2 Check your progress questions Unit 1 Q2, Q4; Unit 2 Q1	Exercises 3.1, 5.1	Worksheets 1.1d, 1.2b, 1.3a, 1.3c, 1.3d, 2.2c
Plan investigative work			
Ask questions and suggest ways to answer them.	Activities 3.3, 4.1, 6.3a		Worksheets 3.3a, 3.3b, 3.3d, 3.5d
Predict what will happen before deciding what to do.	Activities 1.2, 3.1, 3.5, 4.1, 4.2, 5.3, 5.4a, 5.4b, 5.5, 6.3a	Exercises 3.1, 3.3, 3.5, 4.4	Worksheets 1.2b, 2.1c, 2.3c, 2.3d, 3.1, 3.3a, 3.3b, 3.3d, 3.4b, 3.5a, 3.5b, 3.5c, 3.5d, 3.5e, 4.1a, 4.4, 5.3b
Recognise that a test or comparison may be unfair.	Activities 1.1, 3.3, 3.5, 6.3a, 6.3b	Exercise 6.3	Worksheets 2.1c, 2.3c, 2.3d, 3.3d, 3.5b, 3.5d
Obtain and present evidence			
Make suggestions for collecting evidence.	Activities 1.1, 1.2, 4.1, 6.2, 6.3a, 6.3b		Worksheets 1.1d, 2.3c, 3.3d, 3.5d, 4.4
Talk about risks and how to avoid danger.	Activities 1.4, 3.3, 4.1, 4.3, 5.2, 5.3, 5.4a, 5.5, 6.2, 6.3a, 6.3b	Exercise 5.2	Worksheet 3.3d, 3.4b, 5.2

Make and record observations.	Activities 1.1, 1.2, 1.3, 2.1, 2.2, 2.3, 2.4, 3.1, 3.2, 3.3, 3.4, 3.5, 4.1, 4.2, 4.3, 5.1, 5.3, 5.4a, 5.4b, 5.5, 6.2, 6.3a, 6.3b	Exercises 1.1, 1.3, 2.3, 3.2, 3.4, 5.3, 5.5	Worksheets 1.1a, 1.1b, 1.1c, 1.1d, 1.3a, 1.3b, 1.3d, 2.1a, 2.1b, 2.1c, 2.2a, 2.2b, 2.3a, 2.3b, 2.3c, 2.3d, 2.4a, 2.4b, 3.1a, 3.2a, 3.2b, 3.3a, 3.3b, 3.3d, 3.4a, 3.4b, 3.4c, 3.5a, 3.5b, 3.5c, 3.5d, 4.1a, 4.2, 4.3a, 4.3b, 4.4, 5.3a, 5.3b, 5.3c, 5.3d, 5.4a, 5.4b, 5.5, 6.2a, 6.3
Take simple measurements.	Activities 1.1, 3.3, 3.4, 3.5, 6.2, 6.3b	Exercises 6.3	Worksheets 1.3a, 2.1c, 2.3, 3.3a, 3.3b, 3.3d, 3.5a, 3.5b, 3.5d, 6.2a, 6.3
Use a variety of ways to tell others what happened.	Activities 1.3, 1.4, 2.1, 2.2, 2.4, 3.1, 3.5, 4.2, 5.2, 5.3, 6.2	Exercises 1.3, 2.1, 3.1, 3.4, 3.5, 4.2, 5.3, 5.5	Worksheets 1.2b, 1.3b, 1.3d, 1.4, 2.1a, 2.1b, 2.1c, 2.2a, 2.2c, 2.3b, 2.4a, 2.4b, 3.1a, 3.5a, 3.5b, 3.5e, 4.1b, 4.2, 5.3b, 5.3c, 5.3d, 5.4a, 5.4b, 6.2a, 6.3
Consider evidence and approach			
Make comparisons.	Activities 1.1, 2.1, 2.2, 2.3, 2.4, 3.1, 3.3, 3.4, 4.1, 5.4a, 5.4b Check your progress question Unit 6 Q1	Exercises 1.3, 1.4, 2.1, 2.3, 2.4, 3.1, 3.2, 3.3, 3.5, 4.3, 5.3, 5.5, 6.1, 6.3	Worksheets 1.1a, 1.1b, 1.3b, 1.3c, 2.1a, 2.1b, 2.1c, 2.2a, 2.3a, 2.3b, 2.3c, 2.3d, 2.4a, 2.4b, 3.1, 3.2b, 3.3b, 3.3c, 3.3d, 3.4a, 3.4b, 3.4c, 3.5b, 3.5d, 4.1a, 4.2, 4.3b, 5.1, 6.1a, 6.1b, 6.2a, 6.2b, 6.3
Identify simple patterns and associations.	Activities 1.1, 2.4, 3.3, 3.4, 3.5, 4.3, 4.4a, 4.4b, 5.4a, 5.4b, 6.1, 6.2, 6.3a, 6.3b Check your progress questions Unit 4 Q3, Unit 5 Q3, Unit 5 Q4, Unit 6 Q3	Exercises 1.4, 2.1, 2.3, 3.1, 3.3, 4.3, 4.4	Worksheets 1.4, 2.1c, 2.2c, 2.3a, 2.3b, 2.3c, 2.3d, 2.4b, 3.2b, 3.3c, 3.4b, 4.2, 4.3b, 6.1a, 6.1b, 6.2a, 6.2b, 6.3
Talk about predictions (orally and in text), the outcome and why this happened.	Activities 3.1, 4.1, 4.2, 5.4a, 5.4b, 5.5		Worksheets 2.3c, 2.3d, 3.3d, 4.1a, 4.4
Review and explain what happened.	Activities 3.4, 4.2, 4.4b, 5.4a, 5.5, 6.2 Check your progress question Unit 1 Q1, Q4; Unit 4 Q2	Exercises 1.3, 2.1, 2.3, 3.1, 3.3, 3.5, 4.2, 5.3, 5.5	Worksheets 1.3c, 3.1, 3.2b, 3.3b, 3.3c, 3.3d, 3.4b, 3.5c, 4.3a, 5.3a, 5.5

Background knowledge

Different plants and animals live in different local environments. There are also differences in the number of species that live in different environments. You should be able to identify different local environments such as wet and dry areas.

In Stage 1, learners were taught that plants need light and water to grow, and that animals need the right type of food and water to live. This unit builds on this knowledge. It discusses how different environments provide food, water and shelter for the living things that live there. Plants and animals are adapted to make the most of the environments in which they live. Learners do not need to know about these adaptations. But they should be able to recognise that the presence (or lack of) water, food and shelter will have an effect on the living things that are found in an environment.

Animals and plants depend on water. Water is essential for life. It enables the seven life processes: respiration, sensitivity, nutrition, reproduction, movement, growth and excretion. Water is present in all animal and plant tissues. The human body is approximately 60% water.

This unit includes a local survey to identify places where people do not look after the environment. You should be able to help learners to identify examples of damage to the environment which are a result of human activity. Environmental damage is not just caused by industry in urban areas. In rural areas, fertilisers may run off fields into water courses – this causes an overgrowth of plant material which reduces the nutrients in the water for animals that live in it. Chemicals can pollute rural waterways as easily as they pollute urban ones. If humans build on flood plains, then not only are the buildings at risk from flooding, but the natural flow of the river is disturbed and habitats are destroyed. If wild flowers are picked, the population may be reduced as the life cycle of the plants is disturbed. Learners need to understand how they can care for the environment. You should be able to guide the learners as they consider ideas. You might direct them to organisations and resources which can offer ideas, information and suggestions. This is a good opportunity to develop the scientific enquiry skill of using simple information sources.

Weather consists of the temperature, the hours of sunshine, the precipitation (rain, sleet and snow) and the wind. Other atmospheric occurrences are a result of weather. For example, rainbows are a result of rain and sunshine. The Learner's Book does not include activities that involve measurements of, for example, rainfall or temperature. However, you can include these if you feel that it is appropriate for your learners. You should be familiar with the devices used for such measurements such as thermometers, rain gauges, and anemometers (these measure wind speed).

There are different types of clouds. Cirrus clouds are very high in the atmosphere and consist of ice particles. They are thin and wispy. Cumulus clouds look puffy and can be white or grey. They are usually lower in the sky and consist of water droplets. Stratus clouds look like a blanket in the sky. Nimbus clouds are dark and will have rain or snow falling from them. When ice or water particles grow, they become heavy and fall. They reach us as rain or, if it is cold, hail, sleet or snow.

When teaching about the weather, it is useful to be able to show children published and broadcast weather forecasts. (Again, this develops the skill of using simple information sources.) You need to be familiar with the symbols used on such forecasts. For example, the lines or isobars can tell you about wind speeds (isobars closer together indicate higher wind speeds). High and low pressure systems are massive systems of air, which influence the weather.

In this unit, the word 'climate', often confused with the word 'weather', is not used. Climate is an overall summary of the weather experienced in a region over a long period.

Unit overview

Topic	Number of lessons	Outline of lesson content	Resources in Learner's Book	Resources in Activity Book	Resources in Teacher's Resource
1.1 Different places to live	2	Learners compare different environments.	Activity 1.1 Compare two different places (SE) (L) (Ex) (Su)	Exercise 1.1 (SE) (Su)	Worksheet 1.1a (SE) (Su) Worksheet 1.1b (SE) (L) (Ex) Worksheet 1.1c (SE) (Su) Worksheet 1.1d (SE) (Ex) Resource sheet 1.1a Resource sheet 1.1b (L) (Su)
1.2 Can we care for our environment?	2	Learners make observations in their local environment. They develop ideas to care for the environment.	Activity 1.2 Our environment (SE) (L) (Su) (Ex)	Exercise 1.2 (Su)	Worksheet 1.2a (L) (Su) Worksheet 1.2b (SE) (L) (Ex)
1.3 Our weather	2 Exercise 1.3 and Worksheets 1.3a, 1.3b and 1.3d need to be done over the course of a week. **Note:** plastic bottles for Worksheet 1.3a will need preparing in advance.	Learners find out about the weather. They record a day's weather and keep a weather diary.	Activity 1.3 Today's weather (SE) (L) (Su)	Exercise 1.3 (SE) (Su)	Worksheet 1.3a (SE) (Ex) Worksheet 1.3b (SE) Worksheet 1.3c (SE) Worksheet 1.3d (SE) (Ex)
1.4 Extreme weather	2	Learners find out about different forms of extreme weather. They learn about how weather forecasters use satellites to help them.	Activity 1.4 Keeping safe in extreme weather (SE) (L)	Exercise 1.4 (SE) (Su)	Worksheet 1.4 (L) (Su)
1.5 Check your progress			Questions 1 (SE) (Su), 2 (SE) (L) (Ex), 3 (L) (Ex), 4 (SE) (Ex)		

(Ex) Extension (L) Language (SE) Enquiry (Su) Support

Resource list

- clipboards
- stopwatches
- rulers or tape measures
- rope to measure area with (non-standard units)
- cameras (optional)
- audio recorders (optional)
- large poster paper (a sheet per pair or group)
- transparent plastic drink bottles with the tops cut off
- plastic bricks
- marker pens
- sticks
- strips of paper
- glue
- access to the internet

Topic 1.1 Different places to live

In Activity 1.1 in this topic, learners are asked to identify, and then observe, environments with different conditions. They observe the types of animals (minibeasts are suggested) and plants that live in them. If they compare a dry area with a damp or wet area, or a sunny area with a shady area, they should be able to see a difference or a pattern. A range of other environments are introduced in this topic to draw on other knowledge learners may have and to extend their learning by recognising that the same principles apply to a range of environments.

Learning objectives

- Identify similarities and differences between local environments and know about some of the ways in which these affect the animals and plants that are found there.
- Collect evidence by making observations when trying to answer a science question.
- Use first-hand experience.
- Recognise that a test or comparison may be unfair.
- Make and record observations.
- Make comparisons.
- Make suggestions for collecting evidence.
- Take simple measurements.

Curriculum links

- You should link back to Stage 1, where learners learnt that animals need water and food, and that plants need water and light.

- Links can be made to geography, because learners are studying different environments.

Ideas for the lesson

- Begin by reminding learners that in Stage 1 they learnt about what animals and plants need to live. Learners should be able to say that plants need water and light, and animals need water and food. They also need shelter. Ask the learners to work with a partner to think of as many different types of environment as they can in a short period of time. Take feedback and list ideas on the board.

- Discuss similarities and differences between the environments that the learners identified.

- Use the pictures on page 6 of the Learner's Book to extend the discussion in the previous activity. Discuss the similarities and differences between these environments and talk about how these affect the animals and plants that live in each one. The mangrove swamps are home to many different species (see *Internet and ICT* section for more information about this habitat). Rivers in cooler places also support a wide variety of plants and animals (see *Internet and ICT* section for a description of the wildlife that can be found along one such river.) The savannah is home to large animals such as antelopes, and trees such as palm (see *Internet and ICT* section for more information.)

- Picture 1.1 on the CD-ROM can be used to focus the discussion on the effect of environments on one particular type of living thing: trees. A pine tree can live in cold climates because it is able to store any available water and sunlight. The small leaves keep water in the plant. This is because the leaves have a small surface area so not much water evaporates from the surface of the leaves. The leaves are very dark green. They contain a high concentration of the substance chlorophyll. This enables them to use the available sunlight to make a store of food (though the process of photosynthesis) very efficiently. In contrast, a tree in the wet, hot, humid rainforest has big leaves with large surface areas for evaporation to take place. A tree in the desert does not have many leaves. It is withered because it does not have sufficient water available to be transported through its trunk to its leaves.

- In Activity 1.1, learners are asked to visit parts of the school site to identify contrasting areas, for example, wet and dry, or sunny and shady. They study and compare the animal and plant life in each environment. (See *Notes on practical activities* section.) Worksheets 1.1a and 1.1b support this activity.

- You might extend the activity above outside the school site to look for other local environments which are different. Learners will again be able discuss ideas when they compare the two areas. They could record their observations of the similarities and differences they find.

- Show the learners pictures of animals that can live in many environments, for example, humans, pigeons and mice. You could also show them other animals that can only live in particular environments, for example, sperm whale and snow leopard. Resource sheet 1.1a provides pictures that you could use. You could ask higher achieving learners to explain why some animals can only live in particular environments. Worksheets 1.1c and 1.1d support this part of the lesson. In Worksheet 1.1c learners compare and sort animals into those that can live in many environments and those that can only live in certain environments – it is more suitable for lower achieving learners. Worksheet 1.1d is more suitable for higher achieving learners. It also asks learners to research other animals that can live in many environments or only in certain environments. Allow learners access to the internet or other simple information sources in order to complete this. Encourage them to make suggestions about how they will gather information.

- Learners could model and communicate ideas by designing a new animal to live in a particular place, for example, a hot desert or a snowy mountain.

- Ask learners to help you make wall displays and/or 3D models of different environments and the plants and animals that live there. Learners could draw some of the plants they found in each of the environments in Activity 1.1. Ask groups to present their work to others.

- Resource sheet 1.1b gives the vocabulary needed for this unit. You could use this to support lower achieving learners. Alternatively, you could use the words to make a wall display relating to this unit.

- Exercise 1.1 in the Activity Book consolidates the learning in this topic. Learners observe pictures of a waterfall and a dry desert environment and consider if they would be good places for animals and plants to live.

Notes on practical activities

Activity 1.1 Compare two different places

Each pair or group will need:
- a clipboard
- a stopwatch or watch
- something to measure size of areas with (could be non-standard units but the areas should be approximately the same size)
- a camera (optional)

Before starting this activity, ask learners what size of animals they think they will see. Guide them to realise that they are more likely to find minibeasts than large animals. Point out that minibeasts are an important part of any environment. Ask learners to suggest which two different places they want to investigate. To make it fair, the areas should be of roughly similar size. Explain this and ask learners how they will measure the areas (they could use rulers, tape measures or a piece of rope).

Prompt learners to think of a question to ask, before they do this activity. A suitable question might be, 'How does the environment affect the number and type of plants and animals that live there?' You could ask learners to predict what they will find before they do the activity.

Learners will collect evidence by making observations. You can discuss with learners how they will record and compare their observations. You could use Worksheet 1.1a (which is most suitable for lower achieving learners) or Worksheet 1.1b (which is most suitable for higher achieving learners) here.

You should encourage learners to observe leaves, minibeasts and so on carefully. But warn learners that plant and animal material can sometimes be harmful.

Check (as far as possible) that the areas that you visit are free from poisonous or stinging plants. Also check for any allergies to plant material, and for hayfever. Make sure that learners wash their hands after the activity. Make sure that learners are well supervised at all times, particularly in areas where there may be vehicles.

Talk about what learners found. Did they find different numbers or types of wildlife in each environment? Higher achieving learners can think about whether the comparison is fair. Did they observe the same size of area? Did they observe each area for the same amount of time? If they found lots of birds and butterflies in one area, did they look as hard as they did in an area where there were not so many birds and butterflies?

If this unit is taught early in the year, this investigation will allow you to assess learners' scientific enquiry skills. You may find that these vary quite markedly in the class.

Internet and ICT

- Learners might take photographs to record their observations and investigations in this topic.

- Learners could make audio recordings to describe their work (for example in Activity 1.1).

- The website www.inchinapinch.com/hab_pgs/marine/mangrove/mangrove.htm has background information about mangrove swamps and the plants and animals that live in them.

- The website www.weyriver.co.uk/theriver/wildlife_2_trees.htm has information about the wildlife around a particular river in the United Kingdom.

- There is information about the wildlife of the savannah here: library.thinkquest.org/26634/grass/Savanna/animal.htm.

- This website has a video of animals in hot, cold, wet and dry environments: www.bbc.co.uk/learningzone/clips/how-have-different-animals-adapted-to-their-habitats/12665.html.

- There is a video which compares woodland, ditch and pond environments here: www.bbc.co.uk/learningzone/clips/woodland-pond-and-ditch-habitats-within-a-garden/2309.html.

Assessment

- You could use the learning objectives for the topic and turn them into 'I can' statements. For example: 'I can identify similarities and differences between local environments,' 'I can talk about some of the ways in which similarities and differences between local environments affect the animals and plants that are found there,' 'I can predict what will happen when deciding what to do'. You could then show these statements to the learners and ask them to say how much they agree with them on a scale of 1 to 5 where, for example, 5 means 'strongly agree' and 1 means 'strongly disagree'.

- Learners can self-assess their work on Activity 1.1. They should say two things that they did well and one thing that they would like to do better next time.

Differentiation

- Support lower achieving learners by pointing to examples of familiar animals and plants in familiar environments. For example, a snail and where it lives will be familiar to some learners. Assist them with vocabulary; you can use Resource sheet 1.1b for this. You could also give learners specific prompts for Activity 1.1; for example, 'Have you looked under that log?' Worksheets 1.1a and 1.1c are particularly suitable for this group of learners.

- Cater for higher achieving learners by giving them a wider range of examples of animals and plants in their environments. Expect them to make a range of suggestions, for example when you ask questions about environments and the animals and plants that live there, and to use science vocabulary accurately. Give them open questions to think about in Activity 1.1 such as 'Where might we find minibeasts?' Worksheets 1.1b and 1.1d are particularly suitable for this group of learners.

Common misunderstandings and misconceptions

- Learners may forget that animals include minibeasts. So they may think that a particular environment does not have any animals in it when, in fact, there are many hiding under leaves and so on. Draw the attention of learners to minibeasts and the important part they play, for example, in breaking down the bodies of dead animals and plants. Can they say what the world would be like without minibeasts?

Homework ideas

- Ask learners to research how hot or cold environments affect the animals or plants which live in these habitats.

- Exercise 1.1 in the Activity Book is a suitable homework activity.

Answers to Activity Book exercise

Exercise 1.1

1 This would be a **good** place for animals and plants to live. There is **a lot of** water. It would be **easy** to find food. It would be **easy** to find shelter.
2 This would be a **hard** place for animals and plants to live. There is **not much** water. It would be **difficult** to find food. It would be **difficult** to find shelter.

Answers to Worksheets

Worksheet 1.1a

Learners draw the animals and plants they found in the two areas observed.

Worksheet 1.1b

Learners draw, count and describe the animals and plants they found in the two areas observed.

Worksheet 1.1c and 1.1d

Animals that can live in many environments	Animals that can only live in certain environments
mouse	sperm whale
human	snow leopard
pigeon	

Topic 1.2 Can we care for our environment?

This topic reminds learners that humans have a large impact on the environment. We can damage the environment and we can care for it. Learners look at the simple things they can do to care for the environment. They learn that humans can have a significant positive impact.

Learning objectives

- Understand ways to care for the environment. Secondary sources can be used.
- Use simple information sources.
- Make and record observations.
- Collect evidence by making observations when trying to answer a science question.
- Use first-hand experience.
- Predict what will happen before deciding what to do.
- Make suggestions for collecting evidence.

Curriculum links

- This topic links to geography because learners are studying the effects of people on the environment.

Ideas for the lesson

- Before teaching this topic, it would be worth enquiring about local or national groups that are concerned about the environment. It may be possible for a local expert or volunteer to visit the school and talk to the learners about local environmental issues. They may provide free materials for children. Alternatively, the learners could write to them, or use Skype. This would allow learners to ask questions, seek answers and develop ideas.

- Use the picture on page 8 of the Learner's Book as a possible starting point for discussion and ideas about environmental issues. You can extend the discussion with Picture 1.2 on the CD-ROM which shows both threats to the environment and ways to care for it.

- In Worksheet 1.2a, learners can think of the ways in which we look after the environment and the ways we harm the environment. They can write or draw about them. Discuss their suggestions with them.

- The illustration in Exercise 1.2 will provide a further opportunity for discussion about ways that human beings harm the environment. Make it clear that we all have an effect. For example, we may not work in a quarry but we all want buildings and roads.

- In Activity 1.2, learners are asked to carry out a survey of the local area to find places where people do not look after the environment. (See *Notes on practical activities* section.) Worksheet 1.2a could also be used as a recording sheet here.

- Using simple information sources such as books, leaflets and the internet, learners could research and suggest ideas of ways to care for the local environment. Worksheet 1.2b supports this. Learners usually have lots of ideas, which you should encourage. Do not be too concerned about practicality. Allow the ideas to flow. Then ask the learners to talk about how some could be carried out and to predict what their effect might be. Ask them to identify things that they could do easily now. Ideas might include reducing litter by using litter bins: learners could suggest ideas for the design and siting of extra bins; they could make posters to persuade others to use the bins. Another idea would be to make simple habitats for minibeasts. There are websites that give help with making minibeast habitats – see the *Internet and ICT* section for details.
- Write a class letter to local, national (and even international) environmental groups to communicate ideas about the local environment. Involve all learners in contributing ideas to this letter. This enables lower achieving learners, who may not find writing easy, to express their ideas verbally. Their ideas are then valued as part of a group writing task.
- Ask the class to meet the headteacher, school council, governors or other school staff. They could ask about this person's or group's opinion on litter or energy issues. At this meeting, learners could present the posters they made for Worksheet 1.2b.

Notes on practical activities

Activity 1.2 Our environment

Each pair or group will need:
- a clipboard
- camera (optional)

Learners will need the opportunity to observe a natural environment, if possible. If you are in an urban area, you may need to organise a trip to the countryside. Or, at least find a space in the town where learners can observe plants and animals (including minibeasts) and how they might be harmed or cared for. A park or riverbank would be suitable (but if you visit a riverbank, you must observe safety rules; do not allow learners to go too close to the water).

Learners could suggest ideas about what they are going to look for before they leave the classroom. Once outside, learners should identify any damage to the local environment. You might point to examples that are not so obvious, for example, dirty water such as pond water, drain water and so on. They should gather evidence in order to answer the question, 'In what ways do humans harm the environment?' They can record their observations in the form of different recordings; for example, video, drawing, audio, writing. Worksheet 1.2a could be used as a recording sheet for this activity.

Discuss with learners how people could take better care of the environment. How could we stop the harm? How could we put things right? What could learners do to help? For example, they could pick up litter, or they could plant trees where trees have been damaged.

Internet and ICT

- Learners might take photographs to record observations in Activity 1.2.
- Learners could make audio recordings to describe their observations and discussions.
- The website www.makingyourown.co.uk/make-your-own-wildlife-habitats.html gives ideas on how to make a habitat for minibeasts.
- The website gowild.wwf.org.uk/about tells learners about the World Wide Fund for Nature (WWF) 'Go wild' club, WWF environmental campaigns, and ways that they can take action to help care for our environment.

Assessment

- Can learners describe ways to care for the environment? You could tell them about an event when the environment was damaged by human activity, for example, a fire or an oil spill. Can learners say how the damage could have been avoided?
- Can learners explain why their actions have a positive effect? For example, putting litter in bins means it is not on the streets. Learners might list the ways that littering has a bad effect on the environment. They might then explain how they will not drop litter and the effect that will have.

- Learners can assess each other's work in Activity 1.2. Did all learners notice the same things? How well did they record their observations? Did they put their use of simple information sources in this topic to good use?

Differentiation

- Support lower achieving learners by asking them to find just two examples of harm to the environment in Activity 1.2. Guide them with questions such as 'Is litter helpful to wildlife?' Then prompt them to explain their answers. Pair this group of learners with higher achieving learners to do research in this topic. This group can be asked to draw their observations.

- Cater for higher achieving learners by expecting them to find other examples of harm to the environment in Activity 1.2 and to suggest ways in which these examples could be turned around. Challenge them to explain why these actions will have a positive effect.

Common misunderstandings and misconceptions

- Learners may feel that they cannot have much effect on the environment on their own. Ask learners to discuss and to consider that small actions made by many people have a big effect.

- Learners may not value the natural world. They may see humans as more valuable than other living things. You could explain, as learners may not realise, that damage to the environment will eventually have a negative impact on humans.

Homework ideas

- Exercise 1.2 in the Activity Book is a suitable homework activity.

Answers to Activity Book exercise

Exercise 1.2

Answers to Worksheets

Worksheet 1.2a

Learners draw and write about the harm they saw in their local environment.

Learners draw and write about how people could look after their local environment better.

Worksheet 1.2b

Learners draw and write about things that could be done to help care for the local environment and how the environment might improve.

Learners make a poster showing ways to improve the environment.

Topic 1.3 Our weather

This topic introduces weather. Learners are encouraged to observe and record the weather.

Learning objectives

- Observe and talk about their observation of the weather, recording reports of weather data.

- Collect evidence by making observations when trying to answer a science question.

- Use first-hand experience.

- Make suggestions for collecting evidence.

- Make and record observations.

- Use a variety of ways to tell others what happened.

Curriculum links

- The study of weather links to geography.

- If you ask learners to take measurements, for example, of temperature and rainfall, you can link to mathematics. You can also link to mathematics if you ask learners to make a pictogram of the weather data.

- You can link this topic to literacy by considering opposites such as dry and wet, hot and cold, sunny and cloudy, and so on.

Ideas for the lesson

- Use the pictures on page 10 of the Learner's Book to start a discussion about the weather. Picture 1.3 on the CD-ROM provides a few more examples that you might use.

- In Activity 1.3, learners are asked to use first-hand experience to take observations of, and record, today's weather. Encourage them to talk on what they observe about the weather and about yesterday's weather. You might challenge them by asking them to predict what the weather will be like later in the day. The answer to this question will depend on where you are in the world. In some areas, weather such as rainfall is very predictable, but in others it can be very unpredictable and even sophisticated monitoring equipment cannot guarantee accurate short-term forecasts.

- Ask learners to suggest ways to record the weather with symbols. Exercise 1.3 in the Activity Book asks learners to observe the weather for 5 days and to make a weather diary using symbols. They can start this in the lesson with the weather today, and then continue it for the rest of the week, either in school or at home.

- Learners can make additional suggestions for collecting evidence about the weather (which may include taking simple measurements of rainfall or temperature). You could introduce learners to the thermometer as a device used to measure temperature. Perhaps they might make simple measurements using a wall thermometer.

- If you wish learners to take simple measurements of rainfall, they can use Worksheet 1.3a. This worksheet gives instructions on how to make a simple rain gauge and includes a table for recording measurements. (See *Notes on practical activities* section.) You can use non-standard units such as plastic bricks to create the scale.

- Learners could use Worksheet 1.3b to tell others what the weather was like for a week. This worksheet gives a grid for pictograms. Ask learners to use it to record the information that they collect about the weather.

- In Worksheet 1.3c, learners interpret and answer questions about weather data in a pictogram. It could be used to reinforce learning at this point.

- Ask the learners to listen to an audio recording, or watch a video recording, of a weather forecast as a simple information source. You could follow this up by asking them to listen to today's weather forecast and see whether the forecast was correct. You could do this over a period of several days to try and answer the question, 'How reliable is the weather forecast?'

- Ask learners to predict the weather and give a weather forecast. You could set up a role play area where learners can present their weather forecasts. You could record these weather forecasts on video.

- Establish a weather vocabulary poster or dictionary. Resource sheet 1.1b could be useful as a starting point for this. This would allow learners to consider the words and think about what they mean. Weather vocabulary posters could be added to the wall display for this unit.

- Learners can make a simple wind meter by holding up a handkerchief or tissue. Its movement will indicate the strength and direction of the wind. Worksheet 1.3d gives instructions for making a slightly different wind meter and includes a table for learners to describe what the wind they observed was like. (See *Notes on practical activities* section.)

- You might link ideas about the weather to the different environments learners studied in Topic 1.1. Different environments around the world have different weather patterns. (This is not true for different environments in the local area, where the differences are related to factors other than weather, as in the micro-climates created by a bend in a river, a large building and a woodland.) Higher achieving learners could research the weather patterns found in the environments that they met in Topic 1.1.

- Talk about the weather patterns in your own country. If you have learners who have lived in different countries, they could talk about the weather patterns in those countries. Then the class can discuss the differences.

Notes on practical activities

Activity 1.3 Today's weather

Each pair or group will need:
- large poster paper
- a camera (optional)

These simple first-hand observations of the weather are similar to those made by real scientists. This activity focuses on making observations to answer the question, 'What is the weather like today?' Learners are asked to make a poster showing the weather that day. They can draw pictures to represent the weather or they can use or invent symbols. Learners can use the poster to tell others what they found out.

(Additionally, learners can build up and record a useful set of observations over a series of days using Exercise 1.3 in the Activity Book.) Make sure that learners make a record of the type of cloud (if any) that is present in the sky. These observations will be useful in the next topic.

If you decide to ask learners to make measurements, you will also need a rain gauge, a thermometer, and a wind strength meter. (Worksheet 1.3a gives instructions for making a rain gauge; Worksheet 1.3d gives instructions for making a wind meter.)

Worksheet 1.3a Making a rainfall gauge

Each pair or group will need:
● a transparent plastic drink bottle with the top cut off
● some plastic bricks
● a marker pen

You should prepare the plastic bottles in advance. It is not difficult to cut the tops off plastic bottles, but an adult should do it. The cut edge may be sharp. You should cover it with tape so that learners cannot injure themselves on it.

Ask learners to follow the instructions on the worksheet. They should build a tower of plastic bricks the same height as the cut plastic bottle. They should use the tower of bricks as a guide for making the scale for the rain gauge. Ask them to place the bottle next to the tower and then mark on the bottle at the top edge of each brick. Learners could use a ruler instead of a tower of bricks and make a mark on the bottle at every centimetre.

When placing the rain gauges outside, make sure that they are stable and not likely to fall over. You could secure them, for example, with large stones around their base. Once the rain gauge is outside, learners can take readings at intervals at answer the question, 'How much rain has fallen today?' They can record results in a table like the one on the worksheet.

Worksheet 1.3d Making a wind meter

Each pair or group will need:
● a stick
● strips of paper
● glue

Ask learners to follow the instructions on the worksheet. When their stick is ready, encourage learners to observe first-hand and to describe how the paper moves in different conditions (you can simulate this with a fan). For example, in light air movement the paper might move a little, in a light breeze the papers might all move to one side and begin to flutter, and so on. The strips will blow in the opposite direction to that from which the wind is coming.

 Safety Learners must make sure that no one else is close by when they hold their stick.

Learners can record their observations about what the wind was like in the table on the worksheet. Learners can use their descriptions to tell others what happened.

Internet and ICT
● Learners could take photographs to record the weather each day.
● Learners could make audio recordings to describe their observations and forecasts.
● The website www.ehow.com/how_2086258_make-simple-rain-gauge.html gives instructions on an alternative method for making a rain gauge.
● The website www.ehow.com/how_4897104_make-anemometer-kids.html gives instructions on how to make a wind gauge that you could set up in the school grounds. It will need to be constructed by an adult.

Assessment
● A series of photographs or video that learners have taken of different weather types might help them to communicate their ideas about weather. Make an 'I can' statement such as 'I can observe the weather and talk about my observations.' Ask learners then to assess themselves. Can they observe the weather? Can they talk about their observations?
● Can learners record and give reports of weather observations? Are they able to write, draw or say what the weather is like? If learners perform the weather forecast role-play, then you could assess their use of the vocabulary associated with this topic.
● Learners can assess each other's posters

from Activity 1.3. They should give at least two positive comments and then one suggestion about how they could improve the poster.

Differentiation

- Support lower achieving learners by giving them time to observe the weather and to talk about their observations. You could introduce different weather types one at a time for this group. Reinforce the vocabulary of weather using cards from Resource sheet 1.1b.

- Challenge higher achieving learners by asking them to consider and talk about a wide range of weather types. If appropriate, ask this group of learners to take measurements of the weather; for example, temperature, rainfall, wind strength. Worksheets 1.3a and 1.3d will support these activities. You might introduce wind direction to this group. You will find compass cards on Resource sheet 6.2 (page 174 of this guide). These could be used with this group of learners.

Common misunderstandings and misconceptions

- Learners may not link weather to aspects such as cloud cover and wind direction.

Homework ideas

- Exercise 1.3 in the Activity Book could be done at home. Remind learners that the diary can include the weather at the weekend.

Answers to Activity Book exercise

Exercise 1.3

Learners create their own weather diary.

Answers to Worksheets

Worksheet 1.3a

Learners make a rainfall gauge and take their own rainfall measurements.

Worksheet 1.3b

Learners create their own weather pictogram.

Worksheet 1.3c

1 10 days
2 6 days
3 It was probably summer because there were a lot of sunny days.

Worksheet 1.3d

Learners make a wind meter and write descriptions of the wind.

Topic 1.4 Extreme weather

In this topic, learners think about the effects of extreme weather.

Learning objectives

- Observe and talk about their observation of the weather, recording reports of weather data.

- Use simple information sources.

- Talk about risks and how to avoid danger.

Curriculum links

- The study of weather links strongly to geography. In geography, learners find out more about the range of weather in different places and about how weather is formed.

Ideas for the lesson

- Learners can discuss the weather illustrated in the pictures on page 12 of the Learner's Book. Picture 1.4 on the CD-ROM provides two more examples to discuss.

- Show learners videos of extreme weather conditions (see the websites suggested in the *Internet and ICT* section). Discuss how people can keep safe in these weather conditions.

- In Activity 1.4, learners make a poster about one type of extreme weather, how to keep safe in it and what to wear. (See *Notes on practical activities* section.)

- You could watch a recording of a TV weather forecast or look at a forecast online. Ask learners how weather forecasters 'see' the weather. Can learners talk about how satellites provide pictures of the clouds below? Look at images of the Earth from space. You could also refer to the pictures of the satellite and the hurricane from space in the Learner's Book.

- Exercise 1.4 in the Activity Book asks learners to compare and then match pictures of weather conditions to the appropriate clothing for those conditions. This is reinforced on Worksheet 1.4.

Notes on practical activities

Activity 1.4 Keeping safe in extreme weather

Each pair or group will need:
- access to the internet
- large poster paper

Learners are asked to do some research, using simple information sources, on one type of extreme weather. For example, they could choose hurricanes, tornados, heavy rainfall or heat waves. They are then asked to make a poster that tells people, for example younger learners, what to wear and how to keep safe (and avoid danger) in the weather that they choose. Learners will need to think about how to present information for a particular audience. You might ask them whether it would be sensible to present the information using many words, for example, or whether pictures would be better. The last website suggested in the *Internet and ICT* section has some information about different types of extreme weather that is suitable for learners. Higher achieving learners should be able to use the information as presented on the website. You may wish to provide a simplified version for lower achieving learners.

Internet and ICT

- The website www.theweatherclub.org.uk/video/vast-cyclone-moves-across-america has a video of storm clouds moving over USA.
- There are some pictures and a short video about extreme weather at this website: education.nationalgeographic.co.uk/education/activity/extreme-weather-on-our-planet/?ar_a=1. The video is very useful. However, the narration may be too advanced. Consider turning the sound off and ask your learners to talk about what they see.
- The website www.theweatherclub.org.uk/video/new-york-under-snow shows a video of heavy snow in New York.
- There are videos of extreme weather at these websites: stormhighway.com/blog2013/july2213a.php www.bbc.co.uk/news/uk-22260836.

- The website www.weatherwizkids.com has learner-friendly information about different types of weather.

Assessment

- Learners can self-assess their poster from Activity 1.4. They could say what they are pleased with and how they could improve it.

Differentiation

- Support lower achievers by providing lots of visual support with images, video and vocabulary. Pictures and video of extreme weather should initiate discussion and interest. You could simplify the information from the websites suggested in the *Internet and ICT* section for this group of learners.
- Challenge higher achieving learners to do more independent research than lower achieving learners for Activity 1.4. This group of learners should also consider the audience for their poster more independently than lower achieving learners.

Common misunderstandings and misconceptions

- Some learners may think that earthquakes and tsunamis are a form of weather. Explain that earthquakes are a sudden movement of the Earth's crust, the surface layer of the Earth, and that these movements are nothing to do with weather.
- Some learners may think that extreme weather is common. Reassure them that this is not the case and that it only happens occasionally throughout the world. You could also tell learners that some places are more prone to experience certain types of extreme weather than others.

Homework ideas

- Learners could ask family and friends about any extreme weather they have experienced. If families have photographs taken during extreme weather, learners could take them into school to show other learners.
- Exercise 1.4 in the Activity Book could be used for homework.

Answers to Activity Book exercise

Exercise 1.4

Answers to Worksheet

Worksheet 1.4

Learners draw themselves wearing clothes suitable for different weather types. Accept any sensible responses.

Topic 1.5 Check your progress

Learning objectives

● Review the learning for this unit.

Ideas for the lesson

● Learners can be asked to answer the questions on the 'Check your progress' pages of the Learner's Book. These questions cover topics from the whole unit. Some answers are ambiguous, which will lead to discussion that will help to assess learners' understanding of this unit.

Answers to Learner's Book questions

1 a dry place: eagle, goat, lion
  b wet place: frog, fish, duck
2 a A
  b More minibeasts and plants live in place A. This is probably because place A has more food, more water and better places for shelter.
3 a Provide more litter bins.
  b Put protection around young trees to prevent them being damaged.
  c Dredge the pond to clear it; provide litter bins around the edge of the pond; fence off areas around the pond banks so people can't get close enough to throw rubbish in to the pond.
4 a It rained on four days: Monday, Tuesday, Wednesday, Friday.
  b Tuesday
  c Thursday
  d There might be 'a little rain' on Saturday. (This is a sensible prediction as it has rained on on most of the preceding days.)

Animal cards

Vocabulary cards: Part 1

measure	
minibeasts	
record	
litter	
sewage	
protect	
temperature	
wind	
rain	
weather	
same	

Resource sheet 1.1b

Vocabulary cards: Part 2

sunny	
cloudy	
warm	
cold	
frosty	
snow	
hail	
extreme	
forecasters	
storm	
research	

Cambridge Primary Science 2

Worksheet 1.1a

Compare two different places

Name: _____ Date: _____

Draw the plants and animals that you found in your two areas.

Area 1

Area 2

Compare two different places

Name: _____ Date: _____

Draw some animals and plants that you found in area 1.

How many plants did you find in this area? _____

How many animals did you find in this area? _____

What was this area like?

You could use one of these words.

| dry | wet | shady | sunny |

_____

Cambridge Primary Science 2

Draw some animals and plants that you found in area 2.

How many plants did you find in this area? _____

How many animals did you find in this area? _____

What was this area like?

You could use one of these words.

dry   wet   shady   sunny

_____

Animals that live in different places

Name: _____ Date: _____

Which animals can live in many environments? Which can only live in certain environments?

Cut out the animals and stick in the right place.

can live in many environments	can only live in certain environments

Cambridge Primary Science 2

Worksheet 1.1d

Animals and their environments

Name: _____ Date: _____

1 Write these animals in the correct list.

human   mouse   pigeon   snow leopard   sperm whale

Animals that can live in many environments	Animals that can only live in certain environments

2 Do some research.

Find five more animals that can be put in each list.

Problems in our environment

Name: _____ Date: _____

Write or draw about the ways we look after the environment and ways we harm the environment.

People harm our environment	People care for our environment

Worksheet 1.2b

Caring for the area around us

Name: _____ Date: _____

1 Talk about things that could be done in your local area to help care for the environment. Write or draw them here.

2 Think about how the environment could get better. Write or draw what you predict might happen here.

3 Make a poster.
In your poster:

   a Tell people about ways to improve the local environment.

   b Tell people what you will do.

   c Suggest what they could do to help.

Making a rainfall gauge

Name: _____ Date: _____

You will need:
- a transparent plastic drinks bottle with the top cut off
- some plastic bricks
- a marker pen

1 Build a tower of plastic bricks the same height as the cut plastic bottle.

2 Put the tower of bricks next to the bottle. Make a mark on the bottle next to the top edge of each brick to make a scale.

3 Put your rain gauge outside. Measure the rain every day for a week. Write the measurement and the day of the measurement in this table. (You can also write in the time if you measure the rain more than once in a day.)

Remember to empty the rain gauge after each measurement.

Worksheet 1.3a

Day and time	Measurement (number of bricks)

Worksheet 1.3b

Weather pictogram

Name: _____ Date: _____

Make a pictogram of the weather for five days.

Use the symbols.

Here is a grid for you to use.

Number of days	cloudy	rainy	sunny	snow	thunder
5					
4					
3					
2					
1					
0					

Weather

Cambridge Primary Science 2

© Cambridge University Press 2014

Worksheet 1.3b

Cut out these symbols and stick them on to your pictogram.

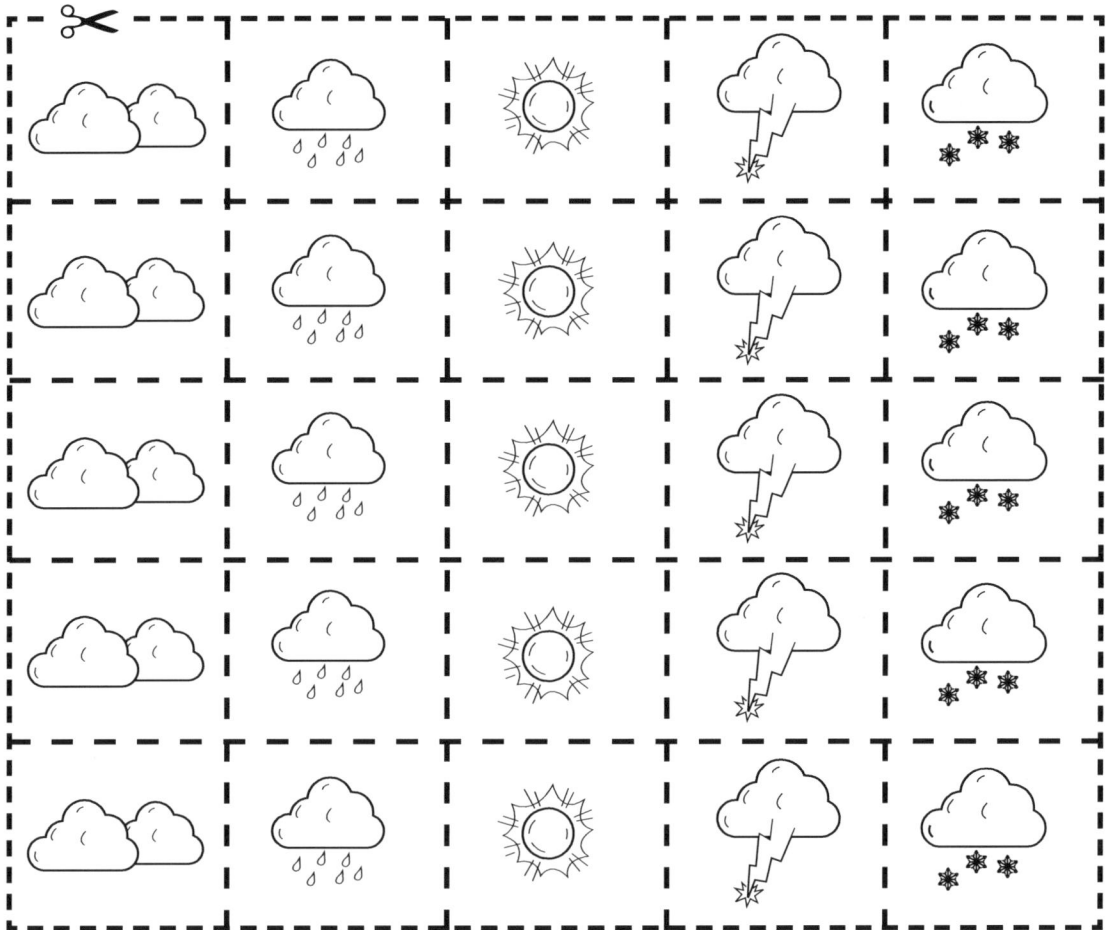

A month of weather

Name: _____   Date: _____

Some learners recorded the weather each day for a month. Look at the pictogram and answer the questions.

The weather at our school in one month.

1   On how many days was there no cloud?   _____

2   On how many days did it rain?   _____

3   Was this month in the summer or winter? Say why you think this.

_____

_____

Cambridge Primary Science 2

Worksheet 1.3d

Making a wind meter

Name: _____ Date: _____

1 Glue one end of each strip of paper to one end of the stick.

2 Take the stick outside. Hold it up in the air.

3 Where is the wind. Which way is the wind coming from?
The strips of paper will blow in the opposite direction.

 **Safety** Make sure that no one else is close by when you hold your stick in the air.

4 How would you describe the wind?

Complete the sentence. Use these words.

not very strong	**quite strong**	**very strong**

Today the wind was

_____

5   Describe the wind. Write down what the wind is like each day for a week.

Day	What is the wind like?

Cambridge Primary Science 2

Worksheet 1.4

The right clothes

Name: _____ Date: _____

Draw yourself wearing the right clothes for the weather in each box.

deep snow	very heavy rain
very hot weather	**very windy weather**

Unit 2

Teaching ideas

Background knowledge

Rocks are naturally occurring solids. They are generally aggregates (mixtures) of various minerals. Rocks cover the surface of the Earth (even the bottom of the oceans is made of rock). There are various classes of rocks. Each class of rock is formed in a slightly different way. Igneous rocks (igneous means 'made from fire and heat') are formed when molten magma from the Earth's core reaches the surface. Granite is a well-known example of an igneous rock. Sedimentary rocks are formed when fragments of rocks settle at the bottom of rivers, for example. Over time they are layered with sand to form a hard rock. Sedimentary rocks may contain fossils. Sandstone is an example of a sedimentary rock. Metamorphic (changed) rocks are rocks that were originally igneous or sedimentary rocks. But they have been changed over time by the movement of the Earth's crust. Marble and slate are both examples of metamorphic rocks.

You may be familiar with rocks used in buildings. These include limestone and marble in floor tiles, slate for roofing and granite in kitchen worktops. You may have chalk sticks in your school. These are made from ground-up chalk rock. Talcum powder is made from ground-up talc rock. Pumice stones are made from pumice rock which is blown out of volcanoes.

Whilst it is useful for you to name some rocks, and your school may have a labelled rock set, it is not vital to do so at this stage. If you want to observe rocks but cannot find the names of them, ask learners to name them as, for example, 'the spotty black and grey rock'.

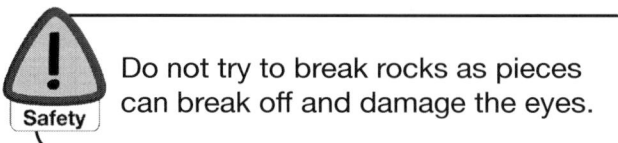

Before undertaking activities involving identifying rocks in your school or elsewhere, make sure you know which items in the area are actually made of rocks. Many materials look like rocks but are in fact man-made materials (rocks are always natural). For example, concrete, construction bricks, tarmac and some types of construction stone are man-made rather than natural rocks; learners may think they are rocks just because they are hard.

The unit looks at other materials and explores a range of natural materials. The difference between natural and man-made materials can sometimes lead to challenging, yet very useful, discussions. For example, is paper man-made when it is clearly made from wood pulp? It is man-made because the paper is made in a factory.

Unit overview

Topic	Number of lessons	Outline of lesson content	Resources in Learner's Book	Resources in Activity Book	Resources in Teacher's Resource
2.1 What are rocks?	1 **Note:** plastic bottles for Worksheet 2.1c will need preparing in advance.	This topic explores the nature of rocks.	Activity 2.1, Comparing rocks (SE) (L) (Su) (Ex)	Exercise 2.1 (SE) (Su)	Worksheet 2.1a (SE) (Su) Worksheet 2.1b (SE) (Ex) Worksheet 2.1c (SE) (Ex) Resource sheet 2.1 (L)
2.2 Uses of rocks	1	Learners look at how rocks are used.	Activity 2.2, Using rocks (SE) (L)	Exercise 2.2 (Su)	Worksheet 2.2a (SE) (Su) Worksheet 2.2b (SE) (Su) Worksheet 2.2c (SE) (L) (Ex) Resource sheet 2.2 (L)
2.3 Soil	1 Worksheet 2.3c will take a few weeks to show results. **Note:** for Worksheet 2.3d, drainage holes will need to be made in the trays in advance.	This topic considers soil.	Activity 2.3, Finding the rock in soil (SE) (Su)	Exercise 2.3 (SE)	Worksheet 2.3a (SE) (Su) Worksheet 2.3b (SE) (Ex) Worksheet 2.3c (SE) (Su) Worksheet 2.3d (SE) (Ex)
2.4 Other natural materials	1	Learners explore a range of natural and man-made materials.	Activity 2.4, Finding materials (SE) (Su)	Exercise 2.4 (L) (Su)	Worksheet 2.4a (SE) (Su) Worksheet 2.4b (SE) (Ex) Resource sheet 2.4 (L)
2.5 Check your progress			Questions 1 (SE), 2 (SE), 3 (L), 4 (Ex), 5 (L) (Su)		

(Ex) Extension   (L) Language   (SE) Enquiry   (Su) Support

Resource list

- hand lenses
- rock samples (available, for example, from www.ukge.co.uk/UK/rocksets.asp?PT_ID=442)
- hard items, such as a metal nails, to scratch the rocks
- water
- simple devices for measuring volume – tall, narrow containers are best (for example, clear, plastic drink bottles with the tops cut off)
- paper towels
- stopwatches
- marker pens
- cameras (optional)
- fossil samples
- a small spade
- different soil samples
- plastic bowls
- water
- plant pots (four per pair or group for Worksheet 2.3c where seeds are grown for a period of several weeks, and four more per pair or group for Worksheet 2.3d)
- soil samples (four different samples per pair or group)
- plant seeds (same type per pair or group)
- sand
- water
- soil (enough of one type of soil for four plant pots per pair or group)
- stones
- trays or junk card boxes with drainage holes (four per pair or group)
- audio recorder (optional)

Topic 2.1 What are rocks?

This topic explains what rocks are. Learners are asked to observe several different rocks.

Learning objectives

- Recognise some types of rocks.
- Use first-hand experience.
- Make and record observations.
- Use a variety of ways to tell others what happened.
- Make comparisons.
- Identify simple patterns and associations.

Curriculum links

- This topic has strong links with geography as both subjects include the study of rocks.

Ideas for the lesson

- Introduce different rocks. You could use the pictures on page 16 of the Learner's Book. Ask learners to describe differences between the rocks.
- Ask learners to discuss what they see in the picture of the quarry on page 17 of the Learner's Book. Can they see different rocks and, perhaps, layers of rocks in the cliffs?
- In Activity 2.1, learners study and compare a set of rock samples. Worksheets 2.1a and Worksheet 2.1b support this activity. (See *Notes on practical activities* section.)
- You can extend Activity 2.1 by considering certain properties of rocks. Worksheet 2.1c supports investigations into the relative hardness of rocks and how well they absorb water. There is an opportunity to develop the skill of identifying patterns here. This is because the hardness and porosity of rocks are related. (See *Notes on practical activities* section.)
- You can have some fun by making edible rocks with the learners (see *Internet and ICT* section for the website with the instructions for doing this).
- You could start a wall display on this unit by displaying some of the learners' drawings of the rocks they observed in Activity 2.1. Resource sheet 2.1 provides the vocabulary for this unit.
- Exercise 2.1 in the Activity Book consolidates what learners will know about the hardness of different rocks. Learners interpret and compare the results of an investigation into the hardness of rocks. They are asked to identify the pattern and explain the results.

Notes on practical activities

Activity 2.1 Comparing rocks

Each pair or group will need:
- a hand lens
- rock samples

Learners can work in groups for this activity. They are trying to answer the question, 'What are the differences between these rocks?' Learners should collect evidence by observing each rock sample carefully. They should compare the rocks and note any differences; for example, colour, whether there are any visible grains or holes, whether there are any patterns in the rocks, and so on. Learners can record their observations by drawing.

Worksheet 2.1a could be used here. This worksheet will support lower achieving learners. Worksheet 2.1b also asks learners to write descriptions of the rocks they observed and could be used for higher achieving learners.

Worksheet 2.1c Looking at the properties of rocks

Each pair or group will need:
- rock samples
- a hand lens
- a hard item such as a metal nail to scratch the rocks
- water
- a simple device for measuring volume – a tall, narrow container is best, for example a clear, plastic drink bottle with the top cut off
- paper towels
- a stopwatch
- a marker pen

If using plastic bottles, you should prepare them in advance. It is not difficult to cut the tops off plastic bottles, but an adult should do it. The cut edge may be sharp. You should cover it with tape so that learners cannot injure themselves on it.

The number of rocks to be tested should be varied according to the ability of the group. For example, higher achieving learners could be given more rocks than lower achieving learners. Make sure the rock samples are labelled (A, B, C and so on) so they can be easily referred to.

Learners should begin the first part of the investigation by predicting which of the rocks will be hardest. They should record their prediction on the worksheet. Then, ask learners to take a nail and try to scratch each rock in turn. Learners should observe what happens in each case. They should compare the rocks and say which they think is the hardest.

The second part of the investigation is to find out which of the rocks will hold the most water. Again, learners should make a prediction before they begin. It might be useful if the learners look carefully at the rocks using a hand lens. Can they see any differences between the rocks that were easy to scratch with the nail and those that were harder to scratch? (Harder rocks will probably have fewer visible 'holes' in their surface.)

Ask learners to put some water into their volume measurer (not up to the top, as the volume will rise when they put the rock in) and mark the water level on the outside of the container.

Then they can put their first rock sample into the water and leave it for 3 minutes. After 3 minutes, learners should take the rock out of the container. Make sure they remove it carefully so that they do not spill any water. Learners should dry the rock with a paper towel. Ask learners to check what the volume of the water is now. If the rock has taken in any water then the volume now will be less than the original volume. Learners should make a mark at the new water level and label this mark 'Rock A'.

If learners then re-fill the container to the original level, they can re-do the investigation for the next rock, and so on. At the end of the investigation, the lowest mark on the container will indicate the rock that absorbed the most water. Learners should compare their results and record which rock held the most water.

Note: this investigation uses very basic equipment and measures so it will not be very accurate. However, it will give an idea about how much water rocks absorb, if any. You might begin a discussion on whether the investigation is fair. An obvious problem is that the rock samples are unlikely to be the same size. So the amount of water absorbed will depend on the size of the samples as well as their porosity. In addition, some learners may not be completely accurate in their marking of the container, or in re-filling the container to the original mark.

Finally, ask learners whether they can identify any pattern in their results. Hardness of rocks is often correlated to their porosity, so learners should see that softer rocks tend to absorb more water.

Internet and ICT

- The website www.kidsgeo.com/geology-games/rocks-game.php has a game to identify rock types. Higher achieving learners may enjoy this.
- There is a rock identification key here: www.bwctc.northants.sch.uk/Learning/Science/Rocks/Key.aspx. You may be able to simplify this for your learners; they have not yet learnt how to use an identification key independently. However, you may find this has useful background information.
- The website www.rocksforkids.com/RFK/howrocks.html introduces different rock types.
- Guidance about what the results of scratch tests mean can be found here: www.rocksforkids.com/RFK/identification.html#Hardness.

- The website www.atlanticeurope.com/sas/3D_Rocks.pdf includes illustrations of some rocks and an example of a simple rubbing test to determine hardness.
- There are instructions and recipes for making edible rocks at this website: www.easyfunschool.com/EdibleRocks.html.
- Various images of buildings are shown at this website: www.sci-eng.mmu.ac.uk/manchester_stone/. If you click on one of the building images, you will be taken to a page with further information about that building, including links to pictures of the quarries from which the stone for that building was quarried.
- There is a virtual tour of a quarry here: www.virtualquarry.co.uk/virtualquarry.htm. Go to 'Quarry face' to see the explosion.

Assessment

- Can learners recognise some types of rocks, for example, sandstone, quartz, slate?
- Learners can assess their own performance in Activity 2.1. What did they do well? What did they have difficulty with? What have they learnt about making observations?
- Learners could also self-assess their performance on Worksheet 2.1c. What did they do well? What did they have difficulty with?

Differentiation

- Cater for lower achieving learners by providing lots of visual and practical stimulus. Give learners opportunities to talk and prompt them to use the language of rocks. Provide lists or cards with rock vocabulary. Resource sheet 2.1 lists the vocabulary for this unit. Worksheet 2.1a is particularly suitable for use with this group of learners.
- Challenge higher achieving learners by asking them to consider a wider range of rocks. When observing rocks, can they talk about the visual appearance and the feel of rocks? Can they use a magnifying glass to observe the fine detail of some rocks? Worksheet 2.1b is particularly suitable for this group of learners. Higher achieving learners may also be encouraged to think of more detail about why the investigation in Worksheet 2.1c is not a fair test.

Common misunderstandings and misconceptions

- Some learners tend to see all rocks as generic rock, rather than recognising there are different types. Remind learners that there are lots of different types of rocks. They have different properties and are used for different things.
- Some learners see stones as something separate from rocks. Tell learners that rocks come in all shapes and sizes, and that boulders, stones, pebbles and gravel are all rock.
- Some learners may think that some rocks such as talc and chalk are not rocks at all. Support learners by introducing them to lots of different examples of rock types.
- Some learners think that some man-made materials, like concrete, are rocks. Explain to learners that rocks are natural, but that not all hard building materials are natural.

Homework ideas

- Exercise 2.1 in the Activity Book could be completed at home.

Answers to Activity Book exercise

Exercise 2.1

1 The softest rock was **sandstone**.
2 The hardest rock was **granite**.
3 The coal and granite damaged the wooden stick because they are **hard**.
4 The limestone and sandstone did not damage the wooden stick very much because they are **soft**.

Answers to Worksheets

Worksheet 2.1a

Learners draw the rock samples they observed.

Worksheet 2.1b

Learners draw and describe the rock samples they observed.

Worksheet 2.1c

Learners record their investigation predictions and observations. Accept any sensible responses.

Topic 2.2 Uses of rocks

This topic looks at how different rocks are used for different purposes, depending on their properties.

Learning objectives

- Recognise the uses of different rocks.
- Use first-hand experience.
- Make and record observations.
- Use a variety of ways to tell others what happened.

Curriculum links

- In Stage 1 learners discovered how materials have different properties. You can build upon that here, introducing the idea that within a single category of material (rock) there can be different varieties with different properties.
- This topic links to geography because both science and geography study rocks.

Ideas for the lesson

- Introduce the topic using the pictures on page 18 of the Learner's Book to show some examples of different rocks. Picture 2.2 on the CD-ROM shows a kitchen scene depicting how some of these rocks, and others, might be used in the home. Some items that learners might think of as rocks are not labelled, such as the walls, sink and crockery. Point out that some things might look like rock while they are not; for example, crockery is usually made of ceramic.
- Activity 2.2 asks learners to look around the school and its grounds for different rocks. They should observe them carefully and record what they find. This will give them the opportunity to develop the science skill of making and recording observations. Worksheet 2.2a supports this activity. (See *Notes on practical activities* section.)
- Ask learners to look for rocks at home. For example, they might observe stone on the floor or outside, talc, chalk, salt. (Salt is often sourced from seawater, as an alternative to rock salt underground – if it is sourced from seawater then it does not count as a rock.) This is another opportunity to develop the science skill of making and recording observations.

Worksheets 2.2b and 2.2c will support this activity. These worksheets are similar but are designed for different groups of learners (see *Differentiation* section). Worksheet 2.2b should be completed at home. In Worksheet 2.2c, learners can practise using simple information sources to research other uses of rocks.

- Ask the learners to make a rock library or museum. This might include rock samples, drawings and photographs of rocks seen in local buildings. The museum could be part of the wall display for this unit. This activity would allow learners to develop science skills such as using first-hand experiences, making and recording observations and making comparisons.
- If learners see rocks containing fossils, make sure you explain that these are animals or plants that lived long ago. These living things died and their bodies were buried underground. Over many, many years the rock around them has formed and left this imprint of the animal. Learners might observe samples or photographs of fossils.
- Exercise 2.2 in the Activity Book reinforces the learning from this topic. It asks learners to make drawings to show how particular rocks are used.

Notes on practical activities

Activity 2.2 Using rocks

Each pair or group will need:
- a hand lens

Take learners on a walk around the school compound or local area. Look for rocks in buildings, walls, roofs, paths and roadways. Take care to distinguish between natural rocks and man-made concrete, mortar and tarmac.

Emphasise that there are natural rocks all around us. Point out that many building materials, such as clay floor tiles, clay roof tiles, bricks, concrete and plastic, are not natural, but man-made. You might want to mention that the soil has rock in it. This includes the obvious stones, but also the smaller grains of sand.

Learners can compare the rocks they find and describe characteristics of some of them, such as colour, patterns and shape, by handling and observing them carefully with a hand lens. Ask learners to talk about why the rocks they observed might have been chosen for those uses. What properties are important?

Learners could make drawings of the rocks, including their colour, or write down what they find out. They can use Worksheet 2.2a to record their observations and tell others what they found.

Internet and ICT

- Take digital photographs of rock samples and, for example, of rocks used in buildings and flooring.
- The website www.gly.uga.edu/railsback/ BS-Main.html has a set of photographs of different buildings and the rock used to construct them.
- As suggested in Topic 2.1, there are more pictures of buildings constructed with rock and of the quarries from which the rock was extracted here: www.sci-eng.mmu.ac.uk/ manchester_stone/.

Assessment

- Can learners talk about why some rocks are used for different purposes?
- On a walk around the school site or local area, can learners point to rocks and say why that rock is being used?
- Learners can assess each other's work in Activity 2.2. Ask them to think about what went well and what they found difficult. You can also encourage them to think about what they learnt from the activity.

Differentiation

- Support lower achieving learners by pointing to obvious features of rocks, by emphasising language and providing lots of opportunities to talk about rocks. Worksheet 2.2b is particularly suitable for this group of learners.
- Cater for higher achieving learners by expecting them to give examples of rocks they have observed and to begin to explain their observations. Worksheet 2.2c is particularly suitable for this group of learners.

Common misunderstandings and misconceptions

- Some learners may see all rocks as hard. Talk about hardness tests and explain that different rocks vary in their hardness. Not all rocks are hard enough to be used for building, for example. Remind learners that sand, talc and chalk are all types of soft rock.

Homework ideas

- Ask learners to talk to family members about rocks they have at home or rocks they have used.
- Exercise 2.2 in the Activity Book could be completed at home.
- Worksheet 2.2b asks learners to look at home for where rocks are used and to draw what they find. It is a suitable homework activity.

Answers to Activity Book exercise

Exercise 2.2

Learners draw something to show how diamond, coal, chalk and sandstone might be used. Any sensible answers should be marked correct.

Answers to Worksheets

Worksheet 2.2a

Learners draw the rocks they found.

Worksheet 2.2b

Learners draw the rocks they found at home.

Worksheet 2.2c

1 We use coal to burn in fires to heat our homes.
2 We use talc to make our skin soft.
3 We use chalk to write.
4 Learners draw other uses of rocks, following their own research. Any sensible answers should be marked correct.

Topic 2.3 Soil

In this topic, learners find out that rocks can be found in soil and they explore soils with different characteristics.

Learning objectives

- Recognise some types of rocks and the uses of different rocks.
- Collect evidence by making observations when trying to answer a science question.
- Use first-hand experience.
- Make comparisons.
- Identify simple patterns and associations.
- Review and explain what happened.
- Make and record observations.

Curriculum links

- A link can be made to Stage 1 where learners found out that plants need light and water. Plants also usually (though not always) need soil. In this topic, learners discover that the quality of the soil can affect how the plants grow.

- This topic links to geography, which features soils as part of the landscape and how the type of soil affects the plants that grow in a place.

Ideas for the lesson

- At the start of the lesson, take the class around the school site to look at the soil in different places. This activity will be collecting evidence to answer the science question, 'How does the type of soil affect the living things in the soil?' If you take a small spade, you or one of the learners can dig small holes to reveal the soil just below the surface. The soil is home for many living things. It is also where the roots of the plants anchor the plant and gain essential nutrients. Picture 2.3 on the CD-ROM illustrates how plant roots sit in the soil. Take soil samples from the different areas back into class. Ask learners to observe the soil carefully. If they use a hand lens, the learners should see a lot of detail. You might refer here to the illustrations on page 20 of the Learner's Book which show things found in the soil.

> **Safety** Take care when handling soil as some children may react to fungal spores released from the soil. Do this work in an airy place with good ventilation and discourage children from directly sniffing soil.

- Learners could draw what they saw at the different sites. They could also compare the soils and note any differences in them, for example, light-coloured sandy or clay soils and darker, richer soil containing organic material. They could also compare the living things that they find in the different soils.

- Explain to learners that there are different layers in the soil. There is often a darker layer at the surface and lighter layers and stony layers deeper down. Use the picture on page 21 of the Learner's Book, and websites such as mocomi.com/soil-profile/, to help learners' understanding.

- In Activity 2.3, learners are asked to put soil samples into a bowl of water and see what rocks they can find in the soil. Worksheets 2.3a and 2.3b support this activity. (See *Notes on practical activities* section.)

- Worksheet 2.3c asks learners to investigate how good different soils are for growing seeds. Note that this investigation takes several weeks for the results to appear so you should carry on with teaching the next topics. (See *Notes on practical activities* section.)

- Worksheet 2.3d asks learners to investigate how quickly soils dry out. (See *Notes on practical activities* section.) You can make this more challenging by offering less support to learners who you think have the capacity to be more independent.

- The ideas in Worksheet 2.3d are explored further in Exercise 2.3 of the Activity Book. Learners are asked to interpret the results of an investigation into the different characteristics of soil.

Notes on practical activities

Activity 2.3 Finding the rock in soil

Each pair or group will need:
- different soil samples
- a plastic bowl of water
- a hand lens

Make sure the soil samples are taken from different areas so that a comparison can be made.

At the start of the investigation, learners should compare the soil samples by observing them carefully. Can they see any differences between them? Then ask learners to put the first sample of soil into a bowl of water. They should rock the bowl to get the water to circulate. The soil sample will separate into its constituent parts.

Learners should observe and describe what happens. Ask learners to repeat this with other soil samples, each time starting with a clean bowl of water. Compare the results from the different soils. Can they talk about how the soils are different?

Learners can record their observations using Worksheet 2.3a (more suitable for lower achieving learners) or Worksheet 2.3b (more suitable for higher achieving learners).

Worksheet 2.3c How good is soil for growing seeds?

Each pair or group will need:
- four plant pots
- four soil samples
- plant seeds
- water

Learners are asked to investigate how good different soils are for growing seeds. You might include a control tray of just sand, as plants should not thrive in this tray. Remember that, initially, all the seedlings will do well because they have sugars and nutrients stored in the seed. However, these will soon be exhausted and the plant will become reliant on the soil for nutrients.

Ask learners to make suggestions about how they should collect evidence in this investigation. Learners should plant some seeds of the same type in each soil sample. Make sure the soil samples are labelled. Remind learners they should give each sample the same amount of water and the same growing conditions (same amount of light) to make the test fair. Ask learners to predict which seeds they think will grow best. They can record their predictions on the worksheet.

If you use seeds which germinate relatively quickly, such as mung beans or alfalfa, then you should see the seeds germinate in a couple of weeks. You will then need to allow another couple of weeks to see what happens to the seedlings. While this investigation is underway, ensure that the learners look after the seedlings. But carry on with teaching the next topic in the meantime. At the end of the investigation, learners can record on the worksheet which soil the seeds grew best in. Ask learners to talk about what happened, to discuss their predictions and their results. Can they suggest why that soil might have been best for the seeds to grow in?

Worksheet 2.3d How quickly do different soils dry out?

Each pair or group will need:
- soil
- four beakers
- stones
- sand
- water
- four trays, or junk card boxes, with drainage holes

In this investigation, learners will collect evidence by making observations to try and answer the science question 'Which type of soil will dry out the quickest'.

Learners can prepare different types of soil by adding different amounts of stones, sand and water to the same amount of soil. Ask learners to make a prediction about what will happen. Which soil do they think will let the most water through to the beaker? The soil samples are then placed on similar trays or junk card boxes with drainage holes cut in them. The drainage holes will need to be made in advance of the activity – each tray will need approximately the same number of holes to ensure the test is fair. Learners should place identical beakers under each sample. Remind learners that the samples must be kept in the same place to ensure the test is fair (it is unfair if the conditions are not the same for all the samples).

Learners should observe and compare how much water drips through to the beaker from each sample. Their observations can be recorded on the worksheet. In considering their results, learners can practise the enquiry skills of identifying simple patterns and associations, talking about predictions, and reviewing and explaining what happened (what was in the soil samples that affected the amount of water in the beaker?).

Internet and ICT

- Learners might take digital photographs of soils they observe, or of stages in investigations.
- The website www.growingthenextgeneration. com/just-for-kids-videos-dirt-on-soil.html includes a video to show how soil is useful for almost all plants and animals and for all sorts of reasons.
- There is a video explaining what a soil profile is here: mocomi.com/soil-profile/.

Assessment

- When looking at different soils, can learners comment on the type of rock particles they observe? Can they talk about, sketch or write about the importance of rock particles in soil?
- Learners can self-assess the practical activities by saying what went well, what they had difficulty with, and what they learnt from each activity.

Differentiation

- Support lower achieving learners by illustrating every stage with real examples and other visual aids. Encourage them to use the vocabulary of rocks and soils. Worksheet 2.3a is particularly suitable for this group of learners.
- Cater for higher achieving learners by having high expectations of the language that they will use and the detail you expect in observations. Give these learners more examples of a range of soils and soil constituents such as very fine grained silty soil and very stony rough soil. Expect them to be able to use reference materials to find out more about rocks in soils. Worksheet 2.3b is particularly suitable for this group of learners.

Common misunderstandings and misconceptions

- Some learners may think that soil is just dirt. Some learners may see soil as inert and just there. They may not appreciate that soil is home to very many living things and is of vital importance to many plants and animals for all sorts of reasons. Play learners the video in the *Internet and ICT* section to help their understanding.

Homework ideas

- Ask learners to list things at home that have grown in soil – for example, salad leaves, vegetables, house plants, plants – or that have come from plants and animals that depend on soil.

Answers to Activity Book exercise

Exercise 2.3

1 stony soil
2 compost
3 The **stony** soil has let most water through because it has **lots of rocks**.
The **compost** has let least water through because it has **few rocks**.

Answers to Worksheets

Worksheet 2.3a

Learners draw what the soil sample looked like in the water.

Worksheet 2.3b

Learners draw and label what their soil samples looked like in the water. They describe the differences in the soil samples.

Worksheet 2.3c

Learners record which soil their seeds grew best in. The answer will depend on the characteristics of the soils used in the investigation.

Worksheet 2.3d

Learners record their observations and explanations of what happened in the investigation. They will see more water in beakers under soil with more stones in. They will see less water in beakers under soil with fewer stones in.

Topic 2.4 Other natural materials

This topic considers other natural materials, not just rocks. It also looks at man-made materials.

Learning objectives

- Know that some materials occur naturally and others are man-made.
- Use first-hand experience.
- Make and record observations.
- Identify simple patterns and associations.

Curriculum links

- This topic links to design and technology as it considers the range of materials in the world.

Ideas for the lesson

- Begin by showing the learners the farmland picture on page 22 of the Learner's Book. Ask them what materials they can see in the picture – which do they think are natural and which are man-made?

- In Activity 2.4, take the children for a walk around the school or local area in order to observe a range of natural and man-made materials. Learners will be able to develop science skills associated with using first-hand experiences. They will also be able to make and record observations. Give learners enough time to look around and talk about the materials they find. Make sure that they are looking at the materials that objects are made from. You can then lead discussions around whether the materials are natural or man-made. Talk about where the natural materials come from – for example, wood comes from trees – and what the man-made materials might be made of. Begin with obvious easy examples of natural materials such as shells, sand, wood, straw, rocks, leaves, potatoes and water. Cotton is natural but cotton fabric is man-made, the same way as paper (previously noted) is man-made. Other examples you might find include cotton fabric, soil, milk and bark, plant material in baskets, iron and bark. Examples of man-made materials are plastic, iron, steel, paint and toothpaste. Introduce more challenge with woven fabric, glass and nylon, for example. Do not worry about whether learners get the harder ones right or wrong. The quality of the discussion is the main thing. You may not be sure what material some objects are made from. This is not a problem – it will allow you to demonstrate positively that no one ever stops learning. You should find a good range of materials used inside and outside the building and in the school grounds. Learners can record the materials they find using Worksheets 2.4a (for lower achieving learners) and 2.4b (for higher achieving learners).

- Learners might sketch some of the materials found in Activity 2.4, take rubbings and take photographs. The rubbings and photographs could be added to the wall display for the topic.

- Make a collection of labelled samples of natural materials – it could be added to the display for this topic. This would allow the development of skills related to observation and handling materials first-hand. Learners could draw pictures of the different samples. These could also be displayed on the wall.

- Look at a collection of books about materials. Can learners find pictures of natural materials? This would help learners to develop science research skills using simple information sources.

- Ask learners to look at an old magazine or catalogue. Can they cut out pictures of natural materials?

- Remind learners what is meant by the term 'man-made'. Ask learners to suggest examples of man-made materials and find some in the classroom. Man-made materials include plastics (which are made from oil), most metals (which are extracted from ores, or rocks; note that gold is a natural material because it is found in a pure state), many fabrics such as polyester, and paper (which is made from wood pulp). You can show Picture 2.4 on the CD-ROM here; it shows a number of common man-made materials linked to the natural materials they are made from. Learners may find some of these examples surprising.

- Look at some objects, each made from a range of materials, such as a bicycle, a sandwich, a bag, a jacket, a sand tray and toys. Ask learners to identify the materials used to make each object and say whether they think the materials are natural or man-made? Can they explain their suggestions? This will help them develop skills linked to making observations.

- Exercise 2.4 in the Activity Book can be used to consolidate learning for this topic.

Internet and ICT

- You could record learner responses on a audio recorder or on www.audioboo.com.
- Learners could take digital photographs of materials.
- The website www.crickweb.co.uk/ks1science. html has sections labelled 'Materials 1' and 'Materials 2' – both provide online games about materials. You could ask learners to identify natural materials.

Assessment

- Can learners say that some materials occur naturally and others are man-made?
- Given a set of materials, can learners identify some of the natural materials? Can they place the natural materials in a set? Can they do the same if given just the names of the materials?
- Give learners the opportunity to self-assess their work in Activity 2.4. What went well? What did they have difficulty with? What did they learn from the activity?

Differentiation

- Support lower achieving learners by providing real examples of different materials. Allow learners to handle the materials and examine them carefully. Some learners may have a good knowledge of materials, but they may find the natural or man-made distinction difficult. Worksheet 2.4a is particularly suitable for this group of learners.
- Cater for higher achieving learners by increasing the challenge of discussion with a wide range of materials and by including more examples that are difficult. You could use foods such as pasta, tomato ketchup and bread. You might ask them to look at objects which are made of several materials, for example, some toys, some furniture and school bags. Worksheet 2.4b is particularly suitable for this group of learners.

Common misunderstandings and misconceptions

- Learners may be confused by examples where an object's name is the same as a material, for example, an iron.
- The word 'material' can cause difficulty if mistakenly used for fabric. Clarify the different terms for learners and correct them if they use the terms inappropriately.
- Take care to distinguish between the objects and the materials from which they are made.

Homework ideas

- Learners might conduct a 'natural materials safari' at home, listing those found.
- Exercise 2.3 in the Activity Book could be completed at home.

Answers to Activity Book exercise

Exercise 2.4

natural: water, sand, wood, metal (gold)

man-made: plastic, paper, glass, ball of wool

Answers to Worksheets

Worksheet 2.4a

Learners draw the materials they found.

Worksheet 2.4b

Learners draw the natural materials they found and where they come from.

Learners draw the man-made materials they found and write what they are made of.

Topic 2.5 Check your progress

Learning objectives

- Review the learning for this unit.

Ideas for the lesson

- Learners can be asked to answer the questions on the 'Check your progress' pages of the Learner's Book. These questions cover topics from the whole unit. Some answers are ambiguous, which will lead to discussion that will help to assess learners' understanding of this unit.

Answers to Learners' Book questions

1 A Marble   B Sandstone
   C Limestone   D Granite
2 A river.
3 It is a very hard, strong, rock. It is also smooth and attractive so often used for decorative buildings.
4 Soil lies on top of the rocks that cover the surface of the Earth. When the large rocks break down into smaller pieces they end up in the soil.
5 wooden table – wood
   rock wall – stone (or rock)
   table salt – salt
   cotton T-shirt – cotton
   woollen jumper – wool

Vocabulary cards: Part 1

Earth	
rock	
sandstone	
granite	
limestone	
quarry	
collect	to find and keep things
diamond	
quartz	

Vocabulary cards: Part 2

marble

slate

soil

sandy

sand

clay

stone

natural

man-made

Looking at rocks

Name: _____ Date: _____

Draw some of your rock samples.

Worksheet 2.1b

Comparing rocks

Name: _____ Date: _____

Draw some of your rock samples.

Were any of your rocks coloured?

_____

Did any of your rocks have spotted bits in them?

_____

How did your rocks feel?

Use these words.

cold   hard   rough   smooth   soft   warm

_____

Worksheet 2.1c

Looking at the properties of rocks

Name: _____ Date: _____

Part 1

1   Look at the rocks. Use a hand lens.

2   Write down which one you think
    will be the hardest.

    I think the hardest rock will be

    _____.

> You will need:
> • rock samples
> • a hand lens
> • a metal nail
> • water
> • a container for water
> • paper towels
> • a stopwatch
> • a marker pen

3   Scratch each rock with a nail. Observe what happens.

4   Compare your observations. Write down what you found.

    Rock _____ was easiest to scratch.

    Rock _____ was hardest to scratch.

Part 2

5   Look at the rocks again.

6   Write down which one you think will hold the most water.

    HINT: Can you see any holes in any of the rock surfaces?

    I think rock _____ will hold the most water.

Cambridge Primary Science 2

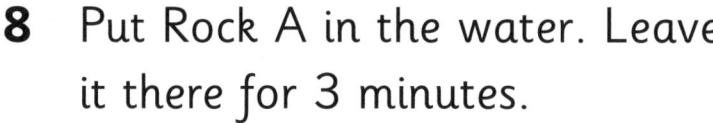

7 Put some water in a container. Draw a line to mark the surface of the water.

8 Put Rock A in the water. Leave it there for 3 minutes.

9 Take the rock out of the water carefully. Dry it with a towel.

10 Draw another line to mark the surface of the water now. Mark the line 'Rock A'.

11 If necessary, add water to the container so the surface is at the first line again. Now repeat the test with the other rocks.

Rock A

12 Which rock held the most water? _____

13 Can you see a pattern in what you found?

HINT: Which was hardest? Which held the most water?

_____

_____

_____

_____

I found these rocks

Name: _____ Date: _____

What rocks did you find? Draw or write about them here.

Rock 1	Rock 2
Rock 3	Rock 4
Rock 5	Rock 6

Cambridge Primary Science 2

Worksheet 2.2b

Rocks in the home

Name: _____ Date: _____

Here are some rocks that you may see at home.

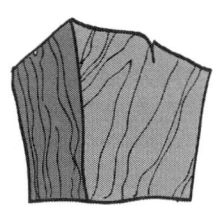 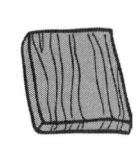    

marble floor tile   rock chalk   drawing chalk   coal burning

Look at home for where rocks are used.

Draw what you find.

I found this. It is made of rock.	I found this. It is made of rock.
I found this. It is made of rock.	I found this. It is made of rock.

Worksheet 2.2c

Using rocks at home

Name: _____ Date: _____

Here are some rocks that you may see at home.

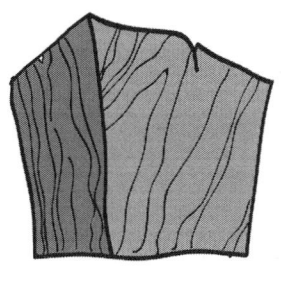

marble

rock chalk

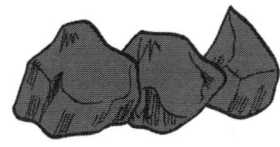

coal

We use some rocks in our homes.

1 Why do we use coal?

_____

2 Why do we use talcum powder?

_____

3 Why do we use chalk?

_____

4 Do some research to find other uses of rocks.

Draw what you find out.

Worksheet 2.3a

Finding the rock in soil

Name: _____ Date: _____

1   Complete the sentence. Use one of these words.

the same   different

Before adding the soil samples to the water, they looked

_____ .

2   Draw what you saw in the first soil sample, after adding
    it to the water.

Worksheet 2.3b

Looking at soil

Name: _____ Date: _____

1 Complete the sentence. Use one of these words.

the same	different

Before adding the soil samples to the water, they looked

_____.

2 Draw and label what you found in the first soil sample, after adding it to the water.

Use these words.

rocks	minibeasts	bits of plants

3 Add some different soil to the water.

Is this soil different from your first soil sample? Write what you found out.

_____

_____

Cambridge Primary Science 2

Worksheet 2.3c

How good is soil for growing seeds?

Name: _____ Date: _____

Look at the pictures
to see what to do.

You will need:
• four plant pots
• four soil samples
• plant seeds
• water

1   In which soil sample do you think the seeds will grow best?

I think the seeds will grow best in soil _____.

2   In which soil sample did the seeds grow best?

The seeds grew best in soil _____.

3   Talk about what happened.

Worksheet 2.3d

How quickly do different soils dry out?

Name: _____   Date: _____

Look at the pictures to see what to do.

1   Say what you think will happen.

2   Try it. Draw what happened in each beaker.

 A    B    C 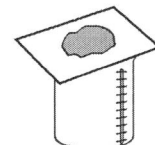   D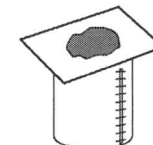

3   Explain what happened.

    Use these words.

more	less	fewer

There was _____ water in beaker _____ because

the soil had _____ stones.

Worksheet 2.4a

Finding materials

Name: _____ Date: _____

Draw what you found.

What sort of material is it? Use these words.

natural   man-made

I found this.	I found this.
It is _____.	It is _____.
I found this.	I found this.
It is _____.	It is _____.

Worksheet 2.4b

Natural and man-made materials

Name: _____ Date: _____

Draw some of the natural materials you found.

Draw where the natural materials come from.

CUP_PS_LB2_2.4.4

Natural	**Natural**
I found this.	I found this.
It comes from here.	It comes from here.
Natural	**Natural**
I found this.	I found this.
It comes from here.	It comes from here.

Cambridge Primary Science 2

Worksheet 2.4b

Draw some of the man-made materials you found.

Write what the man-made materials are made of.

Man-made	Man-made
I found this.	I found this.
It is made of _____.	It is made of _____.
Man-made	**Man-made**
I found this.	I found this.
It is made of _____.	It is made of _____.

Background knowledge

In this unit, learners will observe how different materials respond to simple forces such as pulling and bending. They will learn how materials respond to changes of temperature and that some substances dissolve in water.

Most materials will change shape if sufficient force is applied. In this unit, learners will consider the forces applied when people push and pull on materials. Some materials, such as steel, will change shape and not return to their original shape after the force is removed. Others, such as a rubber band, will return to their original shape after the force is removed. These materials are known as elastic materials. Most elastic materials will break if too much force is applied. This could be dangerous if, for example, a weight being suspended on elastic material falls on a person's foot when the elastic material breaks. You should emphasise that care should be taken when stretching elastic material, as it could break or fly through the air. (Learners should always keep their eyes away from these materials.) As long as learners are supervised, and take care when using these elastic materials, they should not pose a serious risk.

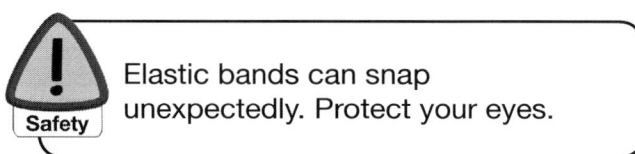

Elastic bands can snap unexpectedly. Protect your eyes.

Elastic can be used to power toys. Energy is stored in stretched elastic and, when the elastic is released, the stored energy can be used to power toys such as cars. Instructions for building such cars are readily available on the internet using the search term 'using elastic to power toys'.

All materials will change if enough heat is applied to them. In this unit, heating is limited to applying just enough heat to have an effect. Most of these changes are reversible. For example, solid water (ice) turns into liquid water when it is heated; if liquid water is cooled it can turn into solid ice. Some examples might be mentioned where the changes are irreversible, for example, burning wood. Ensure learners only heat small samples of each material so that the change is seen more quickly and there is less chance of danger.

Most of the activities in the unit refer to heating because it is easier to heat materials than to cool them in a classroom. Also, the changes are more obvious. Make sure, however, that you do refer to cooling. Learners will be familiar with ice and foodstuffs such as ice lollies and ice cream. You can use these examples to illustrate cooling.

You will be familiar with dissolving, for example, sugar in hot drinks. Take care not to confuse this with melting. Confusing dissolving and melting is a common error or misconception. Ice melts to become water, solid butter melts to become liquid butter. The basic material is the same, but it is in a different state. This is quite different to solid jelly dissolving in water and other examples of dissolving, such as salt and sugar in water. When materials dissolve they seem to disappear. The substances mix on a particle level; the molecules of the material that dissolves mix with the molecules of the solvent. You can no longer see the material because it is no longer present in big 'clumps', though if the material has a colour (like jelly) you can still see the colour. Dissolving is not a chemical reaction – the particles of the dissolving material and the solvent do not chemically combine. The material can be reclaimed by evaporating the solvent; for example, this is how we obtain salt from sea water.

Unit overview

Topic	Number of lessons	Outline of lesson content	Resources in Learner's Book	Resources in Activity Book	Resources in Teacher's Resource
3.1 Materials changing shape	1	Learners look at how materials can change shape by bending, twisting, stretching and squashing. They investigate the effect of squashing.	Activity 3.1 Squashing SE L Su	Exercise 3.1 SE Su L	Worksheet 3.1a SE L Su Worksheet 3.1b L Su Resource sheet 3.1 L Su
3.2 Bending and twisting	1 **Note:** you may need to make dough in advance of this lesson, if you do not have any stored.	Learners look at how bending and twisting affects the shape of materials.	Activity 3.2 Bending and twisting dough SE Su	Exercise 3.2 SE Su L	Exercise 3.2 SE Su L Worksheet 3.2a SE Su Worksheet 3.2b SE Ex
3.3 Fantastic elastic	1 **Note:** you will need to tie handles on to the pots or bags in Activity 3.3 before the lesson.	Learners explore elastic materials. They investigate elastic and the effect of stretching different materials.	Activity 3.3 Looking at elastic bands SE L Su Ex	Exercise 3.3 SE Su L	Worksheet 3.3a SE L Su Worksheet 3.3b SE L Ex Worksheet 3.3c SE Ex Worksheet 3.3d SE Ex Resource sheet 3.3 L Su
3.4 Heating and cooling	1–2	Learners observe, think about and investigate the ways that materials are changed by heating and cooling.	Activity 3.4 Warming foods SE Su Ex	Exercise 3.4 SE Su L	Worksheet 3.4a SE Su Worksheet 3.4b SE Ex Worksheet 3.4c SE Su Resource sheet 3.4 L Su
3.5 Why is the sea salty?	1	Learners observe and investigate how some materials dissolve in water and others do not.	Activity 3.5 Dissolving materials in water SE L Su Ex	Exercise 3.5 SE Su	Worksheet 3.5a SE Su Worksheet 3.5b SE Ex Worksheet 3.5c SE Ex Worksheet 3.5d SE Ex Worksheet 3.5e SE Su Resource sheet 3.5 L Su

3.6 Check your progress			Questions 1 , 2, 3, 4, 5		

 Extension   **L** Language   **SE** Enquiry   **Su** Support

Resource list

- modelling clay
- a collection of materials to squash, like foam, plastic, wood, modelling clay, soap, chocolate, butter, chalk
- cameras (optional)
- audio recorders (optional)
- different types of dough (or dough ingredients: varying amounts of water, salt, cooking oil, flour; sawdust and other additives are optional)
- different-sized elastic bands
- poles
- pots or small bags
- marbles or small stones
- string
- paperclips
- sticky tape
- small interlocking bricks (to measure length)
- various resources to make simple elastic-powered toys (see *Internet and ICT* section)
- thin strips of plastic (for example cut from carrier bags), paper, metal foil and fabric
- thin elastic bands
- thick elastic bands
- springs (for example from ballpoint pens)
- blocks of wood
- a bar of chocolate
- a bowl for melting chocolate in
- container or pan of hot water
- cling film or metal foil
- different food samples for holding (some that will melt and some that will not)
- stopwatches (or access to a clock with a second hand)
- access to an oven and cake-baking materials (optional)
- a good-sized candle (for a demonstration of burning)
- matches or a lighter
- tray or bucket of sand
- foil trays
- strong, plastic, see-through bags
- access to a freezer and liquids that can be frozen

- metal spoons
- wooden pegs or lolly sticks
- candles or night lights
- small samples of different foods for heating with a candle flame such as such as apple, biscuit, chocolate, butter, cheese, pasta, carrot, sand, salt, chalk
- cloths, tissues or water (to clean spoons)
- a small plastic tray with different compartments
- different liquids for freezing such as water, cooking oil, fruit cordial diluted with cooking oil, fruit cordial diluted with water, milk
- salt, sugar and other materials to dissolve such as jelly cubes, flour, rice, sand, talcum powder
- water
- identical beakers
- container (wide and flat preferably)
- a warm place
- liquids for dissolving sugar in such as vinegar, salty water, cola, fruit juice, detergent

Topic 3.1 Materials changing shape

In this topic learners observe familiar materials and they are affected by forces that we can safely create with our hands. They learn about bending, twisting, stretching and squashing. They investigate what happens to materials when they are squashed.

Learning objectives

- Know how the shapes of some materials can be changed by squashing.
- Use first-hand experience.
- Predict what will happen before deciding what to do.
- Make and record observations.
- Make comparisons.
- Collect evidence by making observations when trying to answer a science question.

Curriculum links

- This topic links to science topics such as forces (covered as push and pull in Stage 1) and the study of other characteristics of materials (covered in Unit 4 of Stage 1).

- The topic links to design and technology where learners study and make use of the characteristics of materials, such as rigidity and strength.

Ideas for the lesson

- Use the pictures on page 26 of the Learner's Book to start the lesson. These pictures show modelling clay being bent, twisted, stretched and squashed. You could give each learner a small lump of modelling clay so that they can carry out these actions for themselves.

- In Activity 3.1, learners are first asked to predict the effect of squashing a range of materials. They then squash them and describe the effects of squashing. (See *Notes on practical activities* section.) Worksheet 3.1a will support this activity; learners can draw or write their observations depending on their ability.

- Picture 3.1 on the CD-ROM shows some objects that have been changed by the actions covered in this topic. There are both objects that were created using the actions, and objects damaged by them. Ask learners to identify where instances of squashing, bending, twisting and stretching might have created the shapes they see. You could supplement this with other images.

- Exercise 3.1 in the Activity Book asks learners to compare pictures of squashed balloons and to predict what a balloon will look like when squashed harder than the others. Encourage learners to talk about the association between the shape of the balloon and how hard it is being squashed and to say why they look different.

- Worksheet 3.1b will consolidate the learning from this topic. It asks learners to use the vocabulary from this topic to describe the ways in which the shapes of various objects have been changed.

- Resource sheet 3.1 gives the vocabulary for this unit, which can be used to support lower achieving learners. It could also be used as part of a wall display on this unit. For this topic, you could ask learners to draw pictures to show how the shape of objects can be changed. You could include photographs of models made by the learners using modelling clay.

Notes on practical activities

Activity 3.1 Squashing

Each pair or group will need:

- a collection of materials like foam plastic, wood, modelling clay, soap, chocolate, butter, chalk.

Make sure you have examples of materials that squash easily, materials that are harder to squash, and materials that cannot be squashed by hand. You might also include one or two materials that will break or crumple rather than squash.

Ask learners to follow the instructions in the Learner's Book. Remind them that in science we need a question and we need to make predictions. A suitable question might be, 'How do materials change when we squash them?' Learners should predict what will happen to each material, before trying to squash them. Ask learners to draw what the materials look like before they squash them. Learners can then collect evidence by attempting to squash each material using a finger.

Learners should talk about how the shape of each material changes. Does the material return to its original shape when learners remove their fingers? Ask learners also to make comparisons between the materials. This is a scientific enquiry skill which should be developed at this stage. They should say what happened and whether their predictions were correct.

Worksheet 3.1a supports this activity. Learners can use it to predict how the shape of one of the materials will change when squashed. They can also use it record and compare their observations of the materials before and after squashing in pictures and in simple terms.

Internet and ICT

- Learners might take digital photographs to record the squashing tests on the materials in Activity 3.1.

- Learners might make audio recordings to describe their tests, their predictions and conclusions in Activity 3.1.

- You might use this short video which shows materials being shaped and other changes to materials: www.bbc.co.uk/learningzone/clips/the-use-of-force-to-change-shape/2489.html.

Assessment

- Can learners describe how the shapes of some materials can be changed by squashing, bending, twisting and/or stretching? Worksheet 3.1a is an opportunity to assess this.

- Ask learners to self-assess their work in Activity 3.1. What did they do well? What would they like to improve?

Differentiation

- Support lower achieving learners by providing very clear examples of materials changing shape by being bent, twisted, stretched and squashed. Give examples of materials that can easily and clearly be squashed and ones that do not squash so easily. Assist them in comparing their prediction in Activity 3.1 with what occurred in the test. Resource sheet 3.1 provides the vocabulary for this unit and can be used to support this group of learners. Worksheets 3.1a and 3.1b are particularly suitable for this group.

- Higher achieving learners would benefit from being given a wide range of examples and being expected to use the appropriate language in respect of materials and the investigation in Activity 3.1. Expect them to work more independently. For example, allow them some choice in the materials they test in Activity 3.1 and scope to plan the investigation themselves.

Common misunderstandings and misconceptions

- The word 'material' can cause difficulty if mistakenly used for fabric. Clarify the different terms for learners and correct them if they use the terms inappropriately.

Homework ideas

- Learners could be asked to look around at home and record materials which change shape when squashed.

Answers to Activity Book exercise

Exercise 3.1

1   The drawing should show a balloon being squashed more than the one balloon. (If drawn accurately it would be shown to look wider, as well as flatter. But, this is more than can be expected of learners at this level.)

2   Learners should say that the balloons look different because the size of the push on them is different.

Answers to Worksheets

Worksheet 3.1a

Learners record their predictions, observations and comparisons using drawings.

Worksheet 3.1b

A – stretching
B – twisting
C – bending
D – squashing

Topic 3.2 Bending and twisting

In this topic, learners explore bending and twisting as different ways to change the shape of materials.

Learning objectives

- Know how the shapes of some materials can be changed by bending and twisting.

- Use first-hand experience.

- Use simple information sources.

- Make and record observations.

Curriculum links

- This topic links to science topics such as forces (covered as push and pull in Stage 1) and the study of other characteristics of materials (covered in Unit 4 of Stage 1).

- The topic links to design and technology where learners study and make use of the characteristics of materials, such as rigidity and strength.

Ideas for the lesson

- Use the pictures on pages 28 and 29 of the Learner's Book to start a discussion on how the shape of materials can be changed by bending and twisting. Ask learners whether they think it is easy or hard to bend and twist metal or glass. Ask the same question about balloons. Metals and glass generally need to be heated before they can be bent and twisted; balloons can be bent or twisted at room temperature.

- You could give each learner a small lump of modelling clay so that they can carry out bending and twisting actions for themselves.
- In Activity 3.2, learners are asked to take a lump of dough and bend and twist it into different shapes (see *Notes on practical activities* section). Worksheets 3.2a and 3.2b support this activity. Worksheet 3.2a asks learners to copy shapes with their dough and is suitable for lower achieving learners. Worksheet 3.2b offers extension to this activity by using different types of dough with different characteristics.
- Exercise 3.2 in the Activity Book asks learners to study pictures of materials that have been bent or twisted and decide how their shape has been changed. It will consolidate the learning from this topic.
- You could add to the wall display for the unit by asking learners to draw pictures to show how they changed the shape of the dough in Activity 3.2. You could include photographs of models made by the learners using modelling clay.

Notes on practical activities

Activity 3.2 Bending and twisting dough

Each pair or group will need:
- dough (or dough ingredients: half a cup of salt, one cup of flour, half a cup of warm water, a little cooking oil)

You can make the dough for this activity yourself, but it will need to be done in advance of the lesson.

Basic dough recipe: Add half a cup of salt to one cup of flour in a bowl and stir in half a cup of warm water (you may not need all the water). Add about a tablespoonful of cooking oil. Knead the mix on a floured surface until it takes on the look and consistency of play dough. The dough can be stored in a plastic bag in a refrigerator for up to two weeks.

 **Safety**
Do not allow learners to eat the dough.

Learners should bend and twist dough to make interesting shapes. Worksheet 3.2a gives some shapes that learners can try and copy – it is suitable for lower achieving learners. However, do encourage learners to be creative and make their own shapes as well. Learners can draw the shapes they make using this worksheet.

Worksheet 3.2b offers extension to Activity 3.2 suitable for higher achieving learners (see below).

Worksheet 3.2b Fun with dough

Each pair or group will need:

- four different doughs

This worksheet gives an extension activity to Activity 3.2. Instructions are given on the worksheet. Learners will need four different types of dough, with different characteristics. Label them A, B, C and D.

To make the different doughs for this activity, use the ingredients specified for the basic dough recipe in the Activity 3.2 practical notes above. Vary the amount of water and flour added to the four mixes to make a very stiff mix, a quite stiff mix, a normal mix and a very soft mix. Adding flour to a dough mix makes it drier and it becomes less flexible. It will break more easily when learners try to bend and twist it. Adding water makes the dough more sticky. Learners will find that it is harder to bend and twist as it will simply stick to their fingers. If enough water is added the mixture will become unworkable. You can even use additives such as sawdust. Sawdust makes the dough drier and learners will discover that, when they try to bend or twist it, bits of sawdust will stick out from the main part of the dough.

Make sure you tell the learners what is different about the doughs you give them. Encourage them to compare the doughs and see if they can spot any patterns. How easy is each one to bend and twist? Drier doughs will be harder to work with; very wet doughs will be like slush to work with. Learners can record their observations, and draw the shapes they make, on the worksheet.

Internet and ICT
- Learners might take digital photographs to record the shapes they made with the dough and clay in this topic.
- As for Topic 3.1, you might use this short video which shows materials being shaped and other changes to materials: www.bbc.co.uk/learningzone/clips/the-use-of-force-to-change-shape/2489.html.

Assessment
- Can learners describe how the shapes of some materials can be changed by bending and twisting?

- Ask learners to self-assess their work in Activity 3.2. What did they do well? What would they like to improve?

Differentiation

- Support lower achieving learners by providing very clear examples of materials being bent and twisted. Give examples of materials that clearly bend or twist, and ones that do not bend or twist so easily. Worksheet 3.2a is particularly suitable for this group.

- Support higher achieving learners by giving a range of examples and expecting them to use the appropriate language in respect of materials and the investigations. Challenge them by increasing their autonomy. Worksheet 3.2b is particularly suitable for this group of learners.

Common misunderstandings and misconceptions

- The word 'material' can cause difficulty if mistakenly used for fabric. Clarify the different terms for learners and correct them if they use the terms inappropriately.

Homework ideas

- Exercise 3.2 in the Activity Book would make a suitable homework activity.

Answers to Activity Book exercise

Exercise 3.2

1 This towel has been **twisted**.
2 This pipe has been **bent**.
3 This rope has been **twisted**.
4 This metal has been **bent** to make a hook.

Answers to Worksheets

Worksheet 3.2a

Learners draw the shapes they made out of dough.

Worksheet 3.2b

Learners record which dough was the easiest and hardest to work with. The answer will depend on the exact nature of the doughs used.

Learners draw the shapes they made out of dough.

Topic 3.3 Fantastic elastic

In this topic learners will consider applications for elastic materials. They will investigate the elasticity of different-sized elastic bands and carry out simple stretching tests on various materials.

Learning objectives

- Know how the shapes of some materials can be changed by stretching.
- Collect evidence by making observations when trying to answer a science question.
- Use first-hand experience.
- Ask questions and suggest ways to answer them.
- Talk about risks and how to avoid danger.
- Take simple measurements.
- Recognise that a test or comparison may be unfair.
- Make and record observations.

Curriculum links

- This topic links to other science topics on forces (for example, covered as push and pull in Stage 1) and the study of other characteristics of materials (covered in Unit 4 of Stage 1).
- The topic links to design and technology where learners design and make things using the characteristics of materials, such as elasticity and strength.

Ideas for the lesson

- Learners might look at pictures of applications which use elastic materials. The Learner's Book gives the example of a bungee jumper on page 30. Picture 3.3 on the CD-ROM gives further examples.
- Make a collection of elastic materials in class. Learners could also contribute to this, for example, with elasticated clothing, wristbands, hairbands, shock cord, shirring elastic, tights (perhaps not in every country/ culture) and balloons.
- In Activity 3.3, learners are asked to investigate different elastic bands. (See *Notes on practical activities* section.) Worksheets 3.3a (for lower achieving learners) and 3.3b (for higher achieving learners) support this activity. Learners can record their science question, their prediction, and their observations, and answer questions about the results. Worksheet 3.3b also includes a table to record the results and offers an extension activity.

- Extend Activity 3.3 by encouraging learners to ask science questions about elastic bands. For example, 'Are wide elastic bands stronger?' 'What other materials are elastic?' If you have time, learners could design a simple test.

- Exercise 3.3 in the Activity Book and Worksheet 3.3c reinforce the learning in Activity 3.3. Learners compare and interpret the results from investigations into stretching elastic bands.

- Learners can use elastic bands to flick or push objects across the floor or a table top. They can test different elastic bands, or one elastic band pushing an object across different surfaces. They could ask the question, 'Do thicker elastic bands provide more pushing force?' and investigate it.

- Elastic bands can be used to power simple toys such as elastic-powered planes and cotton-reel rollers. Learners could try different elastic bands and different designs of toys. You will find resources for these on the internet, including how to make 'roller tanks' to power the toys (see *Internet and ICT* section).

- Worksheet 3.3d allows learners to investigate the effects of stretching different materials. Instructions are given on the worksheet and there is a table to record the results. Learners will need to take care to minimise risks. (See *Notes on practical activities* section.) They can predict what will happen, suggest ideas for collecting evidence, say whether the investigation is fair, gather evidence, make comparisons and communicate results and ideas.

Notes on practical activities

Activity 3.3 Looking at elastic bands

Each pair or group will need:
- different-sized elastic bands
- a pole
- a pot or small bag
- marbles or small stones
- string
- paperclips
- sticky tape
- something to measure length such as small interlocking bricks

Help learners to set up the investigation as in the picture in the Learner's Book. Attach an elastic band to a pole using paperclips hooked over the pole. Balance the pole across two chairs and secure it in place using sticky tape.

Then attach a 'weight' to the elastic band, also using a paperclip. To make the 'weight', you can use a yogurt pot, or a small plastic bag, with a handle made of string. You will need to make small holes in the sides of the yogurt pots in order to attach the string. You should do this in advance of the lesson. Add marbles or small stones to the pot or bag, to create the 'weight' that learners will use.

Talk to learners about the pictures in the Learner's Book, the risks of the investigation and how to avoid being hurt. For example: learners should be aware that they must stand so that if the 'weight' falls it does not land on their feet; learners should take care not to over stretch elastic bands so that they break; learners should keep elastic bands away from their eyes.

 Elastic bands can snap unexpectedly. Protect your eyes.

The Learner's Book asks learners to collect evidence to try and answer the question, 'Which elastic band stretches the most?' Learners should try attaching bands of different widths and lengths and comparing them to see how much each elastic band stretches. The mass attached to the elastic bands should be sufficient to make the thickest band stretch a little. Check before the lesson so that you know the number of marbles or stones that will achieve this. Check also that this mass is not sufficient to break the thinnest band. Guide learners with respect to the number of marbles or stones they should use.

Learners should measure the length of each band using a non-standard unit such as small interlocking bricks. They should then add a 'weight' to each band. Remind learners that the same mass should be added to each band to make sure the test is fair. The learners should measure the length of the band now. They could do this by building a tower of bricks on the ground up to the top of the band and measuring the number of bricks down to the bottom of the band. The difference between the length of the band now and the original length is the extension caused by the 'weight'. Learners should find that the thinner the band, the greater the extension.

Worksheets 3.3a and 3.3b can be used to record their observations in this activity. Learners may also record their science question and their prediction on these sheets.

Worksheet 3.3a gives support for recording the results for one band, which you may use if you have little time or for learners who may not complete the activity very quickly. Worksheet 3.3b provides a table to record results for multiple bands. It also introduces the question of what happens to the width of an elastic band when it stretches, as well as the length. Learners should use a very thick band for this question as it will be easier to see the difference. This worksheet is suitable for higher achieving learners.

To extend this activity, you could ask learners to think of other science questions they might ask about elastic and how they might investigate them. You could also ask learners to see what happens if you use bands of the same thickness made of different materials (fabrics) such as cotton, nylon, wool and Lycra. You will need to cut a hole in the fabric to hang a weight through.

Worksheet 3.3d Stretching materials

Each pair or group will need:
- equally thin strips of sheet materials such as plastic (for example cut from carrier bags), paper, metal foil and fabric
- a thin elastic band
- a thick elastic band
- a spring, such as from a ballpoint pen
- a block of wood

Make sure that learners establish a good science question for this activity. For example, 'What happens to materials when they are stretched?' or 'Which material is strongest when we pull it?' Learners should make predictions. They can draw these on the worksheet.

Learners should then design and carry out simple stretching investigations on various materials to collect evidence. Ensure that learners avoid pulling too hard on the materials. Learners could simply pull on the materials individually or in pairs. Alternatively, the investigations here could be based on those in Activity 3.3.

 **Safety** Take care when pulling elastic and springs. Elastic bands can snap unexpectedly. Protect your eyes.

Learners should record the results in the table and compare them against their predictions. Give them the opportunity to talk about what they found so they can practise the enquiry skill of reviewing and explaining what happened.

You could ask learners whether they think their test is fair. If the strips of material are not all the same width it will not be fair. Also, if learners are pulling on the materials themselves, they should think about whether they pulled the same in each case – they might have tried harder with materials that did not stretch easily.

Internet and ICT

- Learners might take digital photographs to record the investigations on the materials.
- Learners might make audio recordings to describe their tests, their predictions and conclusions.
- The following websites show how to make an elastic-powered car: www.ehow.com/how_6387502_make-fast-rubber-band-car.html; www.ehow.co.uk/how_6571110_build-self-propelled-model-car.html.
- This website shows how to make a power 'tank' for elastic-powered toys: www.sycd.co.uk/only_connect/pdf/explore/mini-projects/mini_pupil.pdf.

Assessment

- Ask learners to work in groups to produce some 'can-do' statements for this topic. For example, 'I can describe how some materials behave when they are stretched.' They should then decide how much they agree with the statements: agree, not sure, disagree. This will give you a picture of how confident the learners feel with the content of the topic.

Differentiation

- Support lower achieving learners by making examples very clear and by modelling the scientific language that they are expected to use. You might demonstrate aspects of the investigations. But, ensure that these learners have some decisions to make when planning and carrying out investigations. Challenge them by asking them to say what they found and whether it agreed with any predictions. Worksheet 3.3a is suitable for this group of learners. This group of learners will also find Worksheet 3.3c particularly useful consolidation material.

- Cater for higher achieving learners by expecting them to describe what they observe in detail. Worksheet 3.3b is suitable for this group of learners. They should make predictions and use these in their concluding remarks about what happened, for example in the investigation on Worksheet 3.3d.

This worksheet is particularly suitable for this group of learners because it involves using a method that they have learnt in a different context.

Common misunderstandings and misconceptions

- Learners will often assume that elastic bands are the only elastic materials. They may not understand that very many materials have elastic properties, for example, foodstuffs, fabrics, even their own skin.

Homework ideas

- Ask the learners to find one thing that an elastic band could be used to do at home.
- Exercise 3.3 in the Activity Book would make a suitable homework activity.

Answers to Activity Book exercise

Exercise 3.3

1   D, thick elastic band
2   A and C. (It is not possible to tell from these results which band was weaker.)
3   A (very thin) or C (thin) elastic bands

Answers to Worksheets

Worksheet 3.3a

Learners' measurements of the length of an elastic band before stretching and after stretching. Answers will depend on the thickness of the band and the amount of weight added.

Worksheet 3.3b

Learners' measurements of the lengths of various elastic bands before stretching and after stretching. Answers will depend on the thickness of the bands and the amount of weight added.

Worksheet 3.3c

1   C
2   B
3   Thinner elastic bands stretch more because they are thin and weak.

Worksheet 3.3d

Learners draw their predictions and observations in the investigation to stretch various materials. Drawings will depend on the length, width and type of materials stretched and the amount of force (pull) applied.

Some materials change shape because they have elastic properties. Some materials do not change because they do not have any elastic properties.

Topic 3.4 Heating and cooling

In this topic, learners will test a range of familiar materials, including foodstuffs. Materials will be exposed to different levels of heating and the learners will observe the effects of the heat on the material. Learners also explore the effects of cooling on different materials.

Learning objectives

- Explore and describe the way some everyday materials change when they are heated or cooled.
- Use first-hand experience.
- Make comparisons.
- Identify simple patterns and associations.
- Review and explain what happened.
- Collect evidence by making observations when trying to answer a science question.
- Use simple information sources.
- Make and record observations.
- Take simple measurements.

Curriculum links

- This topic links to Stage 1 when learners looked at the properties of materials. You can make links to Unit 2 as some rocks are formed from other rocks by the action of heat.
- This topic links to food technology where learners would study food preparation including foods that are heated.
- If you use the story *Charlie and the Chocolate Factory* then you can link this topic with language and literacy work.

Ideas for the lesson

- Ask learners if they can find ten different materials in the picture on page 32 of the Learner's Book. How many materials can they find that are being changed by heat? Can they suggest ideas about the ways in which some of the things are changing? Some things are melting; but the egg, for example, is changing in a different way. Learners might also spot that some things, such as pans used for cooking, do not change by heating.

- You could tell them that these things actually will change if you make them *much* hotter.

- Picture 3.4 on the CD-ROM summarises four ways in which materials can change through heat: melting, burning, boiling and changes to the nature of the material. (Burning also involves changes to the nature of the material, but it is not necessary to go into the detail here.) This provides the opportunity for extended discussion with the introduction of heating a liquid until it boils and changes to a vapour or gas. Here water is boiling and changing to water vapour or steam. Ask learners if they have noticed the steam from a kettle when it boils. Tell learners that if the steam is cooled, it will change back to water.

- Demonstrate melting chocolate in a bowl immersed in hot water. Learners can talk about their ideas. What language do we use to describe the solid chocolate? What language do we use to describe the liquid chocolate? How would we describe the change? (For example, it melted, it softened. it turned liquid.) Ask learners whether they can think of questions that they could investigate. Warn learners that liquids like this can get very hot, so they can be dangerous. Exercise 3.4 in the Activity Book could be used at this point. Learners must sort pictures to show whether materials are being changed by heating or cooling.

- Activity 3.4 in the Learner's Book asks learners to investigate warming different foods in their hands. (See *Notes on practical activities* section.) Worksheet 3.4a can be used to record learners' observations.

- You could follow up Activity 3.4 by baking cakes with the learners and talking about the changes in the materials as they are cooked.

- Learners might observe candles burning. Show them the picture on page 33 of the Learner's Book. Then allow them to examine a burning candle close up to see how the hot flame melts the wax and creates a small bath of hot liquid wax. This hot wax soaks into the wick and then burns. It is the wax that is burning, not the wick. This is a very good opportunity for observation first-hand, as learners will notice details. Remind them to use other senses as well as sight, such as hearing and sense of smell.

Observe school regulations about having naked flames in classrooms. Candles should be burnt in trays or buckets of sand with a bucket of sand on hand to put them out if necessary.

- You might place food and other materials in foil trays in warm places around school, such as a windowsill. Make sure you seal food in strong, plastic, see-through bags – learners should not be exposed to the bacteria or spores from micro-organisms on spoiling food. Learners might predict and then observe any changes.

- Worksheet 3.4b is an investigation into heating small samples of foodstuffs (or other materials) over a candle. This will produce rapid changes. Learners can make predictions about what will happen and record observations, which they can compare and communicate to others. Instructions are given on the sheet, along with a table for learners to record their observations in.

- In addition to heating materials, learners should observe materials which cool down after being warmed, for example, liquid chocolate or liquid candle wax returning to a solid state. If you are able to freeze liquids, learners might observe materials before and after freezing. Learners might observe ice from the freezer and the melting of the ice in their hands. This is another good opportunity for observation and discussion about what is happening. Worksheet 3.4c will assist with this activity – instructions are given on the worksheet.

- You might play video extracts of materials being heated; for example, the smelting of iron and the eruption of volcanoes. You can make a link to Unit 2 on rocks by pointing out that some rocks also change by heating and cooling.

- You could read an extract from *Charlie and the Chocolate Factory* by Roald Dahl where chocolate is liquid and runs in a mighty chocolate river.

Notes on practical activities

Activity 3.4 Warming foods

Each pair or group will need:
- cling film or metal foil
- different food samples

- a stopwatch (or access to a clock with a second hand)

Make sure you have some examples of foods that will change in response to body heat and some that will not.

Ask learners to follow the instructions in the Learner's Book. Learners should wrap foods in foil or film, and hold them tightly for a set amount of time. The Learner's Book suggests two minutes, but the exact time should be agreed with the learners before they start. If timing is too difficult for some, you can take control and call out timings to the group or class.

Follow local regulations about handling and preparing food. Make sure that learners wash their hands after the activity.

Some foods should soften so that the change will be observed. Some materials, for example, rice, will not change at this low temperature. This point can be discussed because many learners will have seen rice and other foods cooked at higher temperatures in boiling water. Learners could record their observations in Worksheet 3.4a. Ask learners to use their results to make comparisons between the materials and to try and identify patterns in them. Encourage them to review and explain what happened.

You could extend this activity by asking learners to try holding the materials for longer. Do they notice any difference in what happens? This activity may be more suitable for higher achieving learners.

Worksheet 3.4b Heating materials

Each pair or group will need:
- a metal spoon
- wooden peg or lolly stick
- sticky tape
- a candle or night light
- small samples of different foods such as apple, biscuit, chocolate, butter, cheese, pasta, carrot
- cloth, tissue or water to clean the spoon
- a tray or bucket of sand

The selection of foods suggested includes those that that melt, burn, otherwise change and do not change. Whatever range of samples you use, try to ensure that all of these types of changes can be represented.

You should have on hand a bucket of sand or water on hand to extinguish any flames. This activity has very little risk attached to it, but it is a good opportunity to model cautious behaviour.

Observe school regulations about having naked flames in classrooms. Candles should be burnt in trays or buckets of sand with a bucket of sand on hand to put them out if necessary. Make sure learners keep their faces away from hot materials or materials being heated. Do not heat plastics or paint as these will produce hazardous fumes.

This work should be closely supervised and learners told never to play with flames. You may prefer to do this activity as a demonstration, but do allow learners to do it themselves if possible. Discuss the risks of the investigation with learners, particularly those associated with naked flames.

Tape a wooden peg or lolly stick to each spoon. Learners should hold the wood rather than the spoon to avoid their fingers getting to hot. Ask learners to make predictions about what will happen to the foods when heated. They should then observe the materials at room temperature prior to heating, and the changes they see during heating. Wipe the spoon clean after heating each material. After heating, learners can observe the appearance of the materials as they start to cool again. Learners can use the table in the worksheet to record their observations. Encourage learners to use appropriate science terms such as heating, cooling, melting, solid and liquid to explain what happens.

Worksheet 3.4c Cooling materials

Each pair or group will need:
- a small plastic tray with different sections
- access to a freezer
- a variety of liquids such as water, cooking oil, fruit cordial diluted with cooking oil, fruit cordial diluted with water, milk

Learners should put the different liquid samples in different compartments in the plastic tray. They should put the tray in the freezer and leave it for three hours. At the end of the three hours, they should examine the samples and see what has happened. Learners can use the table in the worksheet to record and compare their observations before and after the liquids are frozen.

Internet and ICT

- Learners might take digital photographs to record the tests on foods and other materials in this topic.
- Learners might make audio recordings to describe their tests, their predictions and conclusions.
- This website shows a video of molten rock flowing from volcanoes: video. nationalgeographic.co.uk/video/environment/ environment-natural-disasters/volcanoes/ volcano-lava/.
- There are some suggestions about other ways in which freezing liquids can be investigated here: www.ehow.com/ list_6022472_science-projects-liquids-freezing.html.

Assessment

- Can learners describe the way some everyday materials change when they are heated or cooled? Ask them to talk about times they have seen food change in the kitchen, for example a raw egg fried in a pan or boiled in water. How does the egg change?
- Ask learners to self-assess the work they did in Activity 3.4. What did they do well? What would they like to improve?

Differentiation

- Support lower achieving learners by prompting them with science vocabulary and using questions to focus their attention. For example, 'Can you see...?' 'Look at the...' 'What do you observe?' 'What have the changes been?' Ask them to model behaviours, such as careful observation, to one another. Challenge them by asking for suggestions and enabling them to do elements themselves.
- Cater for higher achieving learners by challenging them to make detailed observations and to explain what they observe. Can they use the terms 'solid' and 'liquid'? They should be able to consider any aspects of risk and suggest how they can be overcome. The activity described on Worksheet 3.4b is particularly suitable for this group of learners.

Common misunderstandings and misconceptions

- Melting is often confused with dissolving.
- Familiarity with water may mean that learners see melting as something that only happens to solid water (ice). The heating activities in this topic should help learners understand that other materials melt too.

Homework ideas

- Exercise 3.4 in the Activity Book could be completed at home.

Answers to Activity Book exercise

Exercise 3.4

heating: wood, paper, rice
cooling: water, food

Answers to Worksheets

Worksheet 3.4a

Learners draw their observations of each food before they held it and after they held it.

Worksheet 3.4b

Learners draw their observations of different foods before, during and after heating. Very good responses will show detail, for example, about how a liquid has solidified after heating (with a smooth surface or with a rough surface).

Worksheet 3.4c

Liquid	Before freezing	After freezing
water	liquid	solid
cooking oil	liquid	solid/liquid (depending on the oil used and the temperature)
fruit cordial diluted with cooking oil	liquid	solid/liquid (depending on the oil used and the temperature)
fruit cordial diluted with water	liquid	solid
milk	liquid	solid

Topic 3.5 Why is the sea salty?

This topic explains why the sea is salty. It goes on to provide opportunities for learners to observe materials going into solution.

Learning objectives

- Recognise that some materials can dissolve in water.
- Use first-hand experience.
- Predict what will happen before deciding what to do.
- Recognise that a test or comparison may be unfair.
- Make and record observations.
- Take simple measurements.
- Use a variety of ways to tell others what happened.
- Identify simple patterns and associations.

Curriculum links

- The story about why the sea is salty (Resource sheet 3.5) links to literacy. You may also find local myths about why the sea is salty.
- There is a link to Unit 2 when considering the source of sea salt being rocks.

Ideas for the lesson

- Read the myth about the giant who ground salt and made the sea salty from Resource sheet 3.5. Explain that this is a myth – an old story – and that scientists know that the salt has come from salty rocks under the sea, rivers and lakes. This is a good opportunity to talk about a myth which is untrue. What do the learners think? They can talk about different ideas and think about the evidence.
- Learners might be interested to know more about where our salt comes from. Some is evaporated from sea water, some comes from salty water underground. The pictures at the start of this topic on page 34 of the Learner's Book will assist you here.
- From this, you can introduce the idea that the salt is dissolved in sea water. You cannot see it, but it is there. You could encourage learners to think about how they know it is there; that is, because you can taste it.

- In Activity 3.5, learners investigate making solutions in water. (See *Notes on practical activities* section.) Point out that we can drink fresh water, but salt water would make us very ill. Worksheet 3.5a supports the simple activity of dissolving salt in water, and carefully observing what happens. It may be more suitable for lower achieving learners. Worksheet 3.5b supports the more extended activity, which involves trying to dissolve different materials. Higher achieving learners may use it to record their results.
- Picture 3.5 on the CD-ROM has pictures of some everyday solutions. You can use this to show that solutions – liquids with substances dissolved in them – are common, and a big part of our lives.
- In Exercise 3.5 in the Activity Book, learners interpret the results of an investigation into whether salt dissolves faster in warm and hot water. It might be a starting point for another investigation for higher achieving learners, if this has not already been carried out as part of an extension activity to Activity 3.5.
- Worksheet 3.5c is an activity involving evaporating the water from brine to recover the salt. Evaporation is not part of this unit. However, the activity offers useful observation and discussion if you have a little extra time. The observation powerfully supports the idea that the salt does not 'disappear' when it dissolves. Higher achieving learners could be given more independence in this activity.
- If you have extra time, you can extend the content of this unit with the investigation in Worksheet 3.5d. This involves attempting to dissolve sugar in different liquids. This is beyond the requirements of the curriculum. However, it can be used to extend learners and develop scientific enquiry skills, as well as to lay the foundations for understanding of dissolving as a common process that is not limited to water.
- Tell the story of how Roman soldiers were not paid with money but with salt, which was then very valuable and necessary for preserving food. Now salt is often very cheap to buy.
- Worksheet 3.5e consolidates the learning in this topic. Learners are asked to predict what will happen if different substances are stirred into water.

Notes on practical activities

Activity 3.5 Dissolving materials in water

Each pair or group will need:
- salt
- water
- a beaker
- a spoon
- other materials to test like sugar, jelly cubes, flour, rice, sand, talcum powder

First, give learners some salt and some water. Emphasise that salt and water are quite different. What do they observe about these two materials? Ask them to think about what will happen when they mix the materials. Next, allow them to pour some salt into the water and stir the mixture with a spoon. What do they observe during the mixing? The salt appears to disappear. Explain that it does not actually disappear; it is still there but it is no longer visible. It has dissolved. Learners can record their observations on Worksheet 3.5a, which supports this aspect of the activity.

Now, you can repeat this exercise with other substances, as suggested in the Learner's Book, some of which will dissolve and some will not. Make sure fresh water is used for each substance. Learners can use Worksheet 3.5b to tell others what happened using drawings.

You can use this activity to develop different skills. For example, you can introduce ideas of fair testing by discussing whether learners might use the same amount of water and the same amount of substance for each test. This will also give the opportunity to develop measuring skills – the substance can be measured in number of spoonfuls, and the water by filling the beaker to a certain level each time.

You can further extend the activity by asking questions which encourage learners to look at patterns and associations. For example, 'Will a substance dissolve better if you heat the water?' or 'How much (how many spoonfuls) of a substance can you dissolve in a certain amount of water?' You could ask each group to think of a question to investigate and then assist them with deciding what to do. Each group could then report their findings to the rest of the class. Exercise 3.5 will contribute to this; it is also relevant to Learner's Book Check your progress question 5.

Worksheet 3.5c Getting the salt back from salty water

Each pair or group will need:
- water
- salt
- a container
- a spoon
- a warm place, such as a windowsill that gets a lot of sunlight

Learners should make the solution themselves and then place it in a warm place. Make sure you guide learners to use enough salt and water to make a solution where all the salt dissolves. Evaporation will be quicker if the solution is placed in a wide, flat container. Learners should predict what they think will happen. After a few hours, learners can observe the beaker again. They should record their predictions and the results on the worksheet.

The main point of this activity is to observe that the salt can be reclaimed from the solution. In other words, it did not disappear when it dissolved. Talk about this with learners. Can they explain what happened? Learners can write their explanations on the worksheet.

You could extend this activity to answer a science question. For example, 'If you dissolve more salt in the solution will you also get more salt back?' Or, 'If you dissolve more salt will the solution evaporate more quickly?'

Worksheet 3.5d Which liquid will allow most sugar to dissolve?

Each pair or group will need:
- sugar
- liquids such as vinegar, salty water, cola, fruit juice, detergent
- a stopwatch
- a spoon
- identical beakers

Learners should be asked to think of a science question to answer. For example, 'How much sugar will dissolve in different liquids?' Or, 'How quickly will a spoonful of sugar dissolve in different liquids?' The table in the worksheet is set up for the former question, but you can adjust this if needed.

Learners should predict what they think will happen, then make suggestions about how to investigate their question. For example, they might start with equal amounts of the liquids and then add equal amounts of sugar to each liquid, stirring well after each addition. They could keep adding sugar until some solid sugar is visible after stirring well. Ask if the test is fair if they stir the solutions for different lengths of time.

Learners should collect results and then compare the liquids to see which allowed most and least sugar to dissolve. They should think about how they will communicate their findings to others.

Internet and ICT

- Learners might take digital photographs to record the tests in this topic.
- Learners might make audio recordings to describe their tests, their predictions and conclusions.
- There is an alternative investigation, which involves comparing how much sugar will dissolve in water at different heats, at this website: www.sciencekids.co.nz/experiments/dissolvingsugar.html.
- The website www.turtlediary.com/kids-science-experiments/dissolving-experiment.html includes a dissolving experiment.

Assessment

- Do learners recognise that some materials can dissolve in water? Ask learners to describe what happened in Activity 3.5 above. Can learners talk about materials which will dissolve and ones which will not?
- Ask learners to work with others to come up with some simple 'can-do' statements for this topic. For example, 'I can recognise that some materials can dissolve in water,' 'I can take simple measurements,' 'I can use a variety of ways to tell others what happened.' Learners should then assess how well they think they meet these statements: not at all, not really, almost there, completely. This will give you an idea of confidence levels with the content of this topic.

Differentiation

- Support lower achieving learners by enabling them to describe what is happening, particularly when materials seem to have disappeared. They may be very capable at conducting the investigation. However, they may require support, for example, by being reminded what the question is, or in using their observation to formulate a prediction. Worksheet 3.5a is particularly suitable for this group of learners.

- Challenge higher achieving learners by asking them to design and carry out the investigations themselves. Can they devise a question, make a prediction and plan the test? Challenge them with investigating another science question such as 'Does the warmth of the water affect how much salt will dissolve?' (See *Internet and ICT* section.) Worksheet 3.5b is particularly suitable for this group of learners. Worksheets 3.5c and 3.5d could also be used to extend higher achieving learners.

Common misunderstandings and misconceptions

- Many learners confuse melting and dissolving.

Homework ideas

- Learners can ask friends and family at home if they know about salt dissolving into water and what the salt water can be used for.
- Exercise 3.5 in the Activity Book could be completed at home.

Answers to Activity Book exercise

Exercise 3.5

1 hot
2 very cold
3 The salt would take more than 50 seconds to dissolve in iced water.

Answers to Worksheets

Worksheet 3.5a

Learners draw their prediction and the result of their investigation.

Worksheet 3.5b

Learners draw their predictions and the results of their investigation.

Worksheet 3.5c

Learners draw their prediction and the result of their investigation. They also write an explanation.

Most or all of the water will have evaporated.

Worksheet 3.5d

Learners make a prediction and record the results of their investigation.

The liquid that allows most sugar to dissolve will depend on particular liquids used.

Worksheet 3.5e

Learners make reasonable predictions pictures.

Salt – this will dissolve.
Sugar – this will dissolve.
Lots of salt – some salt will dissolve but not all of it.
Sand – this will not dissolve.

Topic 3.6 Check your progress

Learning objectives

- Review the learning for this unit.

Ideas for the lesson

- Learners can be asked to answer the questions on the 'Check your progress' pages of the Learner's Book. These questions cover topics from the whole unit. Some answers are ambiguous, which will lead to discussion that will help to assess learners' understanding of this unit.

Answers to Learner's Book questions

1 a The balloon has been bent and twisted.
   b Some plates are now in small pieces. There are many shapes.
   c Mark correct any words that describe the damage to the car. For example, it has a dent, it is bashed, it is bent.
2 a thick elastic
   b very thin elastic
   c String is not elastic so it would not work.
3 a Chocolate would melt into a liquid.
   b Butter would melt into a liquid.
   c Ice would melt into a liquid. It would become water.
4 a Water would freeze into a solid and go hard. It would become ice.
   b Some types of cooking oil will cool into a solid and go hard in a freezer. Others will remain as a liquid.
   c Liquid chocolate would cool into a solid and go hard.
5 Sand would not dissolve in the water.

Resource sheet 3.1

Vocabulary cards: Part 1

bend	
twist	
stretch	
squash	
change	
shape	
elastic	
heat	

Vocabulary cards: Part 2

hot	
melt	
cool	
liquid	
solid	
ice	
dissolve	
predict	to say what might happen
fair	not unfair

Why the sea is salty

People used to tell this story about why the sea is salty.

Once upon a time all the salt was made by a giant.

He worked all day turning the handle of his salt grinder and out came salt.

People in another land heard about this.

They told the giant that they would make him very rich if he came to their land to grind salt.

He set off on a ship which sailed into a storm.

The giant continued to grind his salt.

The storm grew worse and the ship sank to the bottom of the sea.

The giant is still at the bottom of the sea grinding salt!

This is why the sea is salty.

Squashing

Name: _____ Date: _____

Draw what the materials looked like before squashing.

```



```

Make a prediction. Draw how you think one material will change shape.

```



```

Draw what the materials looked like after squashing.

```



```

Which materials changed shape? Write or draw them.

```



```

Which materials did not change shape? Write or draw them.

```



```

Worksheet 3.1b

Changing shape

Name: _____ Date: _____

In each picture, think about how the shape has been changed.

Use these words.

bending	squashing	stretching	twisting

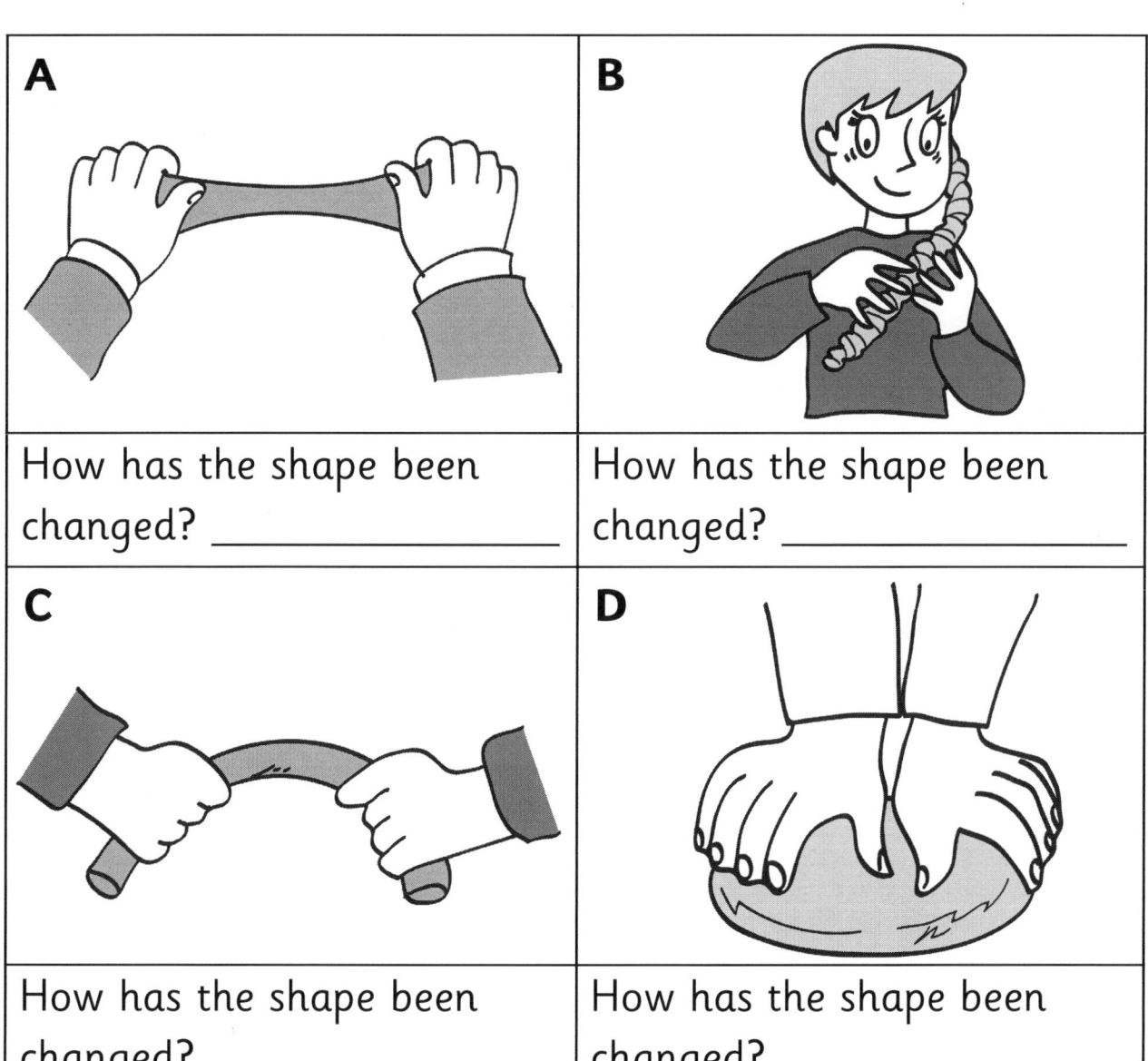

A

How has the shape been changed? _____

B

How has the shape been changed? _____

C

How has the shape been changed? _____

D

How has the shape been changed? _____

Worksheet 3.2a

Bending and twisting dough

Name: _____ Date: _____

Try and make these shapes using your dough.

You will need:
• dough

Make some more shapes. Draw them here.

Cambridge Primary Science 2

© Cambridge University Press 2014

Worksheet 3.2b

Fun with dough

Name: _____ Date: _____

1 Use each dough to make this shape.

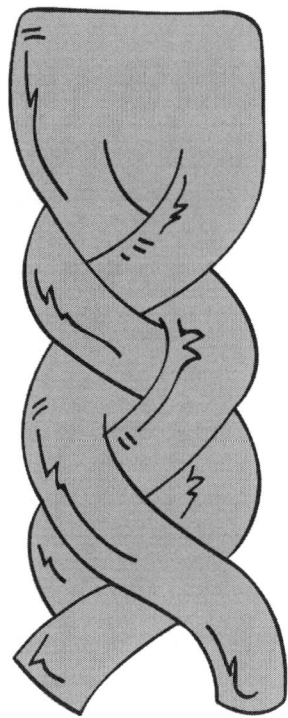

> You will need:
> - four different doughs, labelled A, B, C and D

2 Which dough was easiest to work with? _____

3 Which dough was hardest to work with? _____

4 Choose one of the doughs. Make some more shapes. Draw them here.

Worksheet 3.3a

Looking at elastic bands

Name: _____ Date: _____

My science question is:

_____

Predict what you think will happen. Write your prediction below.

_____

Measure the band before stretching.

The band length is _____ bricks.

Measure the band with the weight attached.

The band length is _____ bricks.

The amount the band stretched is:

length with weight – length without weight = _____ bricks.

Cambridge Primary Science 2

Worksheet 3.3b

Investigating elastic bands

Name: _____ Date: _____

My science question is:

_____

Predict what you think will happen. Write your prediction below.

_____

Measure band A before stretching.

The length of band A is _____ bricks.

Measure band A with the weight attached.

The length of band A is _____ bricks.

The amount band A stretched is:

length with weight – length without weight = _____ bricks.

Do this again with bands of different lengths and widths.

Write what happened in the table on the next page.

Band	Length without weight	Length with weight	Difference in length
A			
B			
C			
D			

Which band stretched the most? _____

What happens to the width of a thick band as it is stretched?

Draw the outline of the unstretched band.

Draw the outline of the band as it is gradually stretched by a larger and larger weight.

Cambridge Primary Science 2

Worksheet 3.3c

Which elastic is strongest?

Name: _____ Date: _____

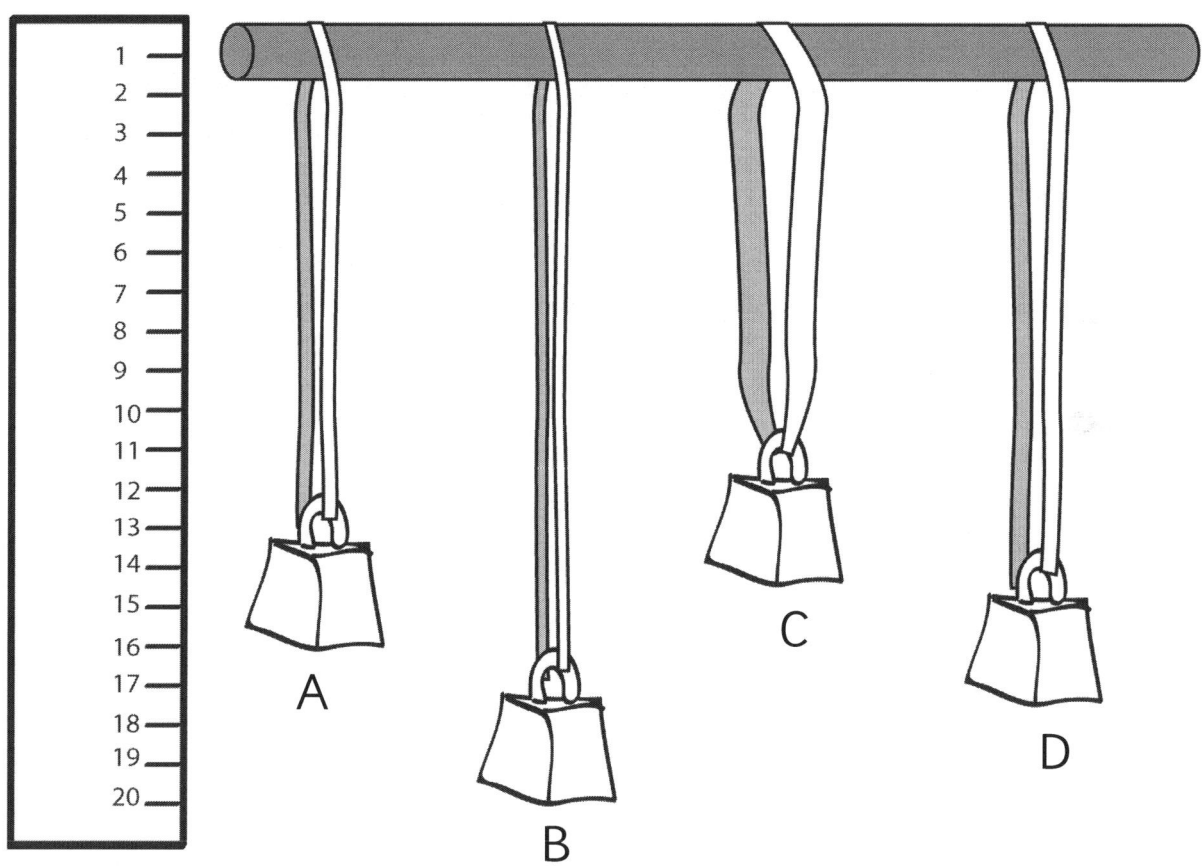

These elastic bands are being tested with four equal weights.

1 Which band is the strongest? _____

2 Which band has stretched the most? _____

3 Why do the thinner elastic bands stretch more?

_____

Worksheet 3.3d

Stretching materials

Name: _____   Date: _____

You will need:
- thin strips of plastic, paper, metal foil, fabric
- a thin elastic band
- a thick elastic band
- a spring
- a block of wood

! Safety Take care when pulling elastic and springs. Elastic bands can snap unexpectedly. Protect your eyes.

Take a strip of plastic.

Draw what you think will happen if you pull on the plastic.

Now hold each end of the plastic and pull.

Draw what happens to the plastic.

Do the same with the other materials.

Draw in the table what you think will happen and what happens to each material.

Cambridge Primary Science 2

© Cambridge University Press 2014

Worksheet 3.3d

What do you think will happen?	What happens?
plastic	plastic
paper	paper
metal foil	metal foil
fabric	fabric
thin elastic	thin elastic
thick elastic	thick elastic
a spring	a spring
a block of wood	a block of wood

Why do some materials change and others do not?

_____

Tell people what you found out.

Worksheet 3.4a

Warming foods

Name: _____ Date: _____

What foods did you test? Write them in the table.

Draw each food in the table before you held it and after you held it.

Food	Before I held it.	After I held it.

Cambridge Primary Science 2

Worksheet 3.4a

Food	Before I held it.	After I held it.

Heating materials

Name: _____ Date: _____

Your teacher will light the candle for you.

Put a small bit of one food on the spoon.

Move the end of the spoon with the food into the candle flame and warm it gently. Make sure you hold the wood at the other end of the spoon so your fingers do not get hot.

What happens to the food?

Draw what you see in the table. Now do the same with other foods.

You will need:
- a metal spoon with a wooden peg or lolly stick taped to it
- candle or night light
- different foods
- cloth, tissue or water to clean the spoon
- a tray or bucket of sand

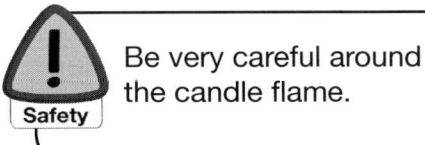

Be very careful around the candle flame.

Safety

Food	Before heating	During heating	After heating

Worksheet 3.4b

Food	Before heating	During heating	Afyer heating

Worksheet 3.4c

Cooling materials

Name: _____ Date: _____

What do the different liquids look like?

Add samples of the different liquids to the different sections in the tray. Put the tray in the freezer. Leave it for three hours.

> You will need:
> - a small plastic tray with different sections
> - a freezer
> - different liquid samples like water, cooking oil, fruit cordial diluted with cooking oil, fruit cordial diluted with water, milk

Describe the liquids before they go in the freezer and after they have been in the freezer. Use these words.

liquid   solid

Liquid	Before freezing	After freezing
water		
cooking oil		
fruit cordial diluted with cooking oil		
fruit cordial diluted with water		
milk		

Cambridge Primary Science 2

© Cambridge University Press 2014

Worksheet 3.5a

Dissolving salt in water

Name: _____ Date: _____

How much salt will you use? _____

Draw the salt.

How much water will you use? _____

Draw the water.

Draw what you think
will happen when you
put the salt into the
cold water and
stir it.

Draw what happens
when you put the
salt into the cold
water and stir it.

Dissolving materials

Name: _____ Date: _____

How much salt will you use? _____

How much water will you mix with the salt? _____

Will you use the same amount of material and the same amount of water for each test?

Draw what you think will happen when you mix each material with water.

What I think will happen.	
salt	sugar
jelly cubes	flour
rice	talcum powder

Cambridge Primary Science 2

Worksheet 3.5b

Draw what happened when you mixed each material with water.

What happened.	
salt	sugar
jelly cubes	flour
rice	talcum powder

Getting the salt back from salty water

Name: _____ Date: _____

Add the salt to the water and stir it well using a spoon.

You will need:
- water
- salt
- a container
- a spoon
- a warm place

Put the salty water in a warm place. Leave it there for a few hours.

Draw what you think will happen.

Draw what happened.

Can you explain what happened?

_____

_____

_____

Worksheet 3.5d

Which liquid will allow most sugar to dissolve?

Name: _____ Date: _____

Use these words to answer the question.

cola	detergent	fruit juice
	salty water	vinegar

Which liquid do you think will allow most sugar to dissolve?

_____

How will you carry out your test to see if you are right?

How much sugar and how much liquid will you use?

How much sugar dissolved in the liquids?

Liquid	Amount of sugar dissolved
vinegar	
salty water	
cola	
fruit juice	
detergent	

Worksheet 3.5e

Materials in water

Name: _____ Date: _____

Look at the pictures below.

What will happen when each spoonful is stirred into the water?

Draw a picture to show what will happen.

water	salt	water	sugar
This is what will happen:		This is what will happen:	
water	lots of salt	water	sand
This is what will happen:		This is what will happen:	

Cambridge Primary Science 2

© Cambridge University Press 2014

Background knowledge

A light source is something that makes light. There are many different sources of light. The most important is the Sun, because this is the source of all our energy on Earth. Most electronic screens produce light. Anything that contains any kind of light bulb also produces light. Older incandescent bulbs, with a thin filament wire, emit light because the wire gets very hot. These are very inefficient because they produce more heat than they do light. They are being phased out in many countries. Fluorescent tubes and compact fluorescent bulbs are more efficient because they produce less heat. They produce light by passing electricity through a gas, which makes the gas glow. Even more efficient are LEDs, or light emitting diodes, which produce even less heat. These can be very small, like the tiny coloured LEDs on the front of computers or mobile phones. But recently, larger single LEDs have been developed that can be used instead of bulbs in torches or bicycle lights. Because they are so efficient, battery life is much better in an LED torch than one with a normal bulb. Other non-electrical sources of light include flames, glow worms, fire flies and objects that are luminous.

Luminous objects glow in the dark. They should not be confused with fluorescent objects that simply look bright in the light. A luminous object can absorb light energy in the light. It can then release the light energy for a limited time in the dark.

Learners often think that the Moon, water, mirrors, other shiny surfaces and high-visibility clothing are also sources of light. However, none of these objects are light sources – they all reflect light rather than make it. The Moon, for example, reflects light from the Sun.

High visibility clothing works in two ways. It is usually made from a combination of fluorescent material, that looks particularly bright when the light, and retro-reflective strips that reflect light very well. The grey-looking retro-reflective strips send the light back in the direction it has come from. So they provide excellent visibility at night when the light from a car's headlights will be reflected from the strips straight back to the driver.

We see objects when light from a source falls on them and scatters in all directions. If some of this light enters our eyes, we can see the object. Learners will be aware that we see with our eyes. But they may not realise that we can only see when light passes though the black pupil, in the centre of the eye, and the lens in the eye. The light forms an upside-down picture of the object we are looking at on the retina at the back of the eye. Light-sensitive nerve cells in the retina send signals through the optic nerve to the brain.

Learners may be interested to notice that the pupil changes size for different light conditions. When it is very bright, the pupil becomes very small. But when it is quite dark, the pupil will become larger to let in as much light as possible.

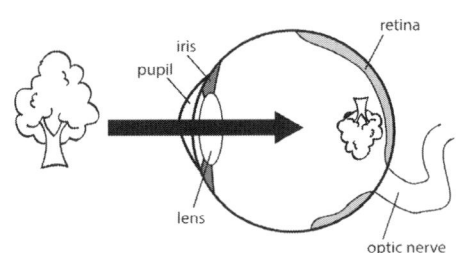

Learners may be aware that some animals can see better than humans in low light levels. Animals that do this tend to have larger pupils, to let in more light, and more sensitive nerve cells in the retina. No animals can see in absolute darkness.

Shadows form when objects block light. Opaque objects (objects that block light completely) do this most effectively. Translucent objects (objects that let some light through but that cannot be seen through, such as paper) will also form dark shadows because they block most of the light that falls on them. Transparent (see-through) objects often form a much darker shadow than expected. This is because they do block some light and they scatter some light, which is how we can see them. A perfectly transparent object would have no shadow and would be invisible.

Be sensitive to learners with limited or no vision in this unit. Many partially sighted learners will be able to explore different light sources. However, they may have difficulty seeing shadows due to the lack of contrast. Blind learners will still be able to feel the light from the Sun as warmth on their skin. They may also be able to detect some heat from other light sources.

 **Safety** Tell learners not to touch their eyes as this can cause infection or damage. Learners should be warned never to look directly at bright light sources, especially the Sun, as this can damage their eyes. Explain to learners how sunlight can cause sunburn, which can be painful and can cause skin cancer. Talk with learners about how to avoid sunburn by covering up bare skin and using sunscreen products on their skin.

Unit overview

Topic	Number of lessons	Outline of lesson content	Resources in Learner's Book	Resources in Activity Book	Resources in Teacher's Resource
4.1 Light sources	2	Learners find out about different light sources.	Activity 4.1 Is it a light source? SE	Exercise 4.1 L	Worksheet 4.1a SE Worksheet 4.1b SE Su Resource Sheet 4.1a Resource sheet 4.1b L Su
4.2 Darkness	1–2 **Note:** you will need to make dark boxes before the lesson.	Learners investigate seeing in the dark.	Activity 4.2 Can you see in the dark? SE Su Ex	Exercise 4.2 SE L	Worksheet 4.2 SE Resource sheet 4.2 L Su
4.3 Making shadows	1	Learners observe shadows carefully and explore how they are made.	Activity 4.3 Making shadows in the Sun SE Su	Exercise 4.3 SE L Su	Worksheet 4.3a SE Worksheet 4.3b SE Resource sheet 4.3 L Su
4.4 Shadow shapes	1–2 **Note:** you may need to make a screen before the lesson if you do not have one.	Learners explore how to change shadows and make shadow puppets.	Activity 4.4a Making shadow puppets SE Activity 4.4b SE Ex	Exercise 4.4 SE L	Worksheet 4.4 SE Su Resource Sheet 4.4
4.5 Check your progress			Questions 1 L , 2 SE , 3 SE		

 **Ex** Extension  **L** Language **SE** Enquiry **Su** Support

Resources

- thick, dark fabrics to make a 'Dark Den'
- masking tape
- selection of objects to test such as books, shiny paper, mirrors, bottles of water, rulers, pencils, high-visibility jackets, and light sources such as torches, luminous toys, mobile phones
- black paper for night-time drawings
- photographs of cities at night
- a cardboard box with lid (one per pair or group)
- small object to go in the box (one per pair or group)
- black card
- craft knife
- sticky tape
- camera (optional)
- torch (one per pair or group)
- selection of small objects to make shadows with such as erasers, small 3D shapes, model people, other small toys
- chalk
- overhead or data projector
- screen made from white cotton fabric fixed to wooden (or card) frame
- light source to light up the screen
- coloured, transparent plastic
- opaque card
- scissors
- glue

Topic 4.1 Light sources

In this topic, learners explore light sources.

Learning objectives

- Identify different light sources including the Sun.
- Collect evidence by making observations when trying to answer a science question.
- Use first-hand experience.
- Predict what will happen before deciding what to do.
- Talk about risks and how to avoid danger.
- Make and record observations.
- Make comparisons.
- Talk about predictions (orally and in text), the outcome and why this happened.
- Ask questions and suggest ways to answer them.
- Make suggestions for collecting evidence.

Curriculum links

- This topic could be linked to Art when learners make night-time pictures.

Ideas for the lesson

- Find out what learners know about light sources by asking them to talk about or draw pictures of where light comes from. Explain that the term 'light source' means something that makes light. Ask learners to identify things that make light in the classroom. Talk with learners about common misconceptions such as mirrors, windows and the Moon. Light does come from these things but either they reflect light or light comes through them. They do not make light. Use the picture on page 38 of the Learner's Book to stimulate the discussion.
- Picture 4.1 on the CD-ROM provides some further examples, including some more complex ones which may extend the discussion.
- Read Activity 4.1 with learners then let them go into the 'Dark Den' in pairs to investigate light sources. Worksheet 4.1a could be used to support this activity.
- Take learners on a hunt for light sources around the school. Look for lamps, fluorescent lights, computer or phone screens, LEDs on computers and screens. Back in class, ask learners to draw some of the light sources they have seen.
- Learners can use Worksheet 4.1b to sort objects into those that are light sources and those that are not. **Note:** learners may not realise that stars are light sources. This may lead to an interesting discussion. (See *Common misunderstandings and misconceptions* section for more guidance.)
- Learners could use paints or pastel crayons on black paper to create night-time pictures. They could include many light sources such as lights from houses, stars, fireworks or car headlights. Show learners photographs of cities at night to give them ideas. Alternatively, learners could cut out the pictures on Resource Sheet 4.1a and stick them onto black paper to make a night time picture.
- Learners can complete Exercise 4.1 in the Activity Book. This asks learners to colour in only the light sources in the picture.
- Resource sheet 4.1b gives some vocabulary for this unit. Use it to support lower

achieving learners, or use the cards as part of a wall display on this unit. You could use the learners' pictures from this topic to start the display.

Notes on practical activities

Activity 4.1

Each pair or group will need:
- fabric to make a dark place
- objects to test such as a book, shiny paper, a mirror, a bottle of water, a torch, as well as other light sources.

To make a dark place, or a 'Dark Den', cover a table with dark and thick fabric, as these are better at blocking out the light. The more layers of fabric you can use the darker the den will be. Any gaps will let in a surprising amount of light, so make sure that the entrance has a large overlap and the pieces of fabric are long enough to reach the floor. Masking tape can be used to secure the fabric to the table if necessary.

Ask learners to work in pairs, using first-hand experience, to investigate whether something is a light source or not. Things that reflect light, like mirrors, will look dark in the Dark Den where there is no light for them to reflect. Light sources will make light in the Dark Den.

Give learners a selection of objects. Include torches and other light sources such as bicycle lights, toys or sticky stars that glow in the dark (luminous) and maybe a small screen such as that on a mobile phone or tablet computer. It is also important for learners to test everyday objects that are not light sources, such as rulers, pencils and books, as well as objects that are confusing, such as high-visibility jackets or belts, plastic mirrors and other bright shiny materials. Talk with learners about safety and why they cannot test candles or matches.

 It is not safe to allow learners to test candles or matches.

Allow learners to compare the objects and ask them to predict which of the objects are light sources before they enter the Dark Den. They should then collect evidence by making observations in the Dark Den.

Ask learners to decide what to do once inside the Dark Den. Ask them to think about whether it is more scientific to test the light sources one at a time or all at once. Ask learners to make suggestions about how to test the objects that they think are not light sources and to decide what to do. Make sure learners understand that they need to look at these objects with all the light sources turned off. You could agree with learners a short list of instructions and display them on a poster outside the Dark Den. Learners can use Worksheet 4.1a to record their predictions and the comparisons and observations they make results. After the investigation, talk with learners about how their predictions compare with their results.

Internet and ICT

- There are some photos of cities at night at these websites: www.smashingmagazine.com/2008/11/09/60-beautiful-examples-of-night-photography-2/ and www.ephotozine.com/article/city-photography-at-night-14967.
- Learners can investigate different light sources at this website: www.bbc.co.uk/schools/scienceclips/ages/5_6/light_dark.shtml.
- The website www.wimp.com/amazingstrike/ includes a short video of lightning (another light source).

Assessment

- After Activity 4.1, ask learners to show each other their recorded results and talk about what they found out. Ask them to look for similarities and differences in the results. Any differences may need to be tested again. This encourages learners to carry out the scientific enquiry objective of using a variety of ways to tell others what happened.

Differentiation

- Make vocabulary cards to help lower achieving learners with the new vocabulary in this topic. Learners can use these at tables. Alternatively, the cards can be made into a class display. Make use of Resource sheet 4.1b here.
- Talk with higher achieving learners about the association between light and heat. Most light sources get very hot. This is because when materials get very hot they give off light. Metal and rock give off red/orange light when very hot.

Common misunderstandings and misconceptions

- Many learners will think that the Moon is a light source. Some learners may think that shiny surfaces such as mirrors and water are light sources. Explain that light does come from all of these but they do not make light. The light is made by a light source and then it is reflected or bounced off the surface of these objects. Learners can test this by taking mirrors or a bottle of water into the Dark Den with no light source. They will look dark.

- Some learners may not realise that stars are light sources. Explain that our Sun is a star but it is much closer. The other stars are very similar balls of burning gases. But other stars are much, much further away.

Homework ideas

- Exercise 4.1 in the Activity Book.
- Worksheet 4.1b.

Answers to Activity Book exercise

Exercise 4.1

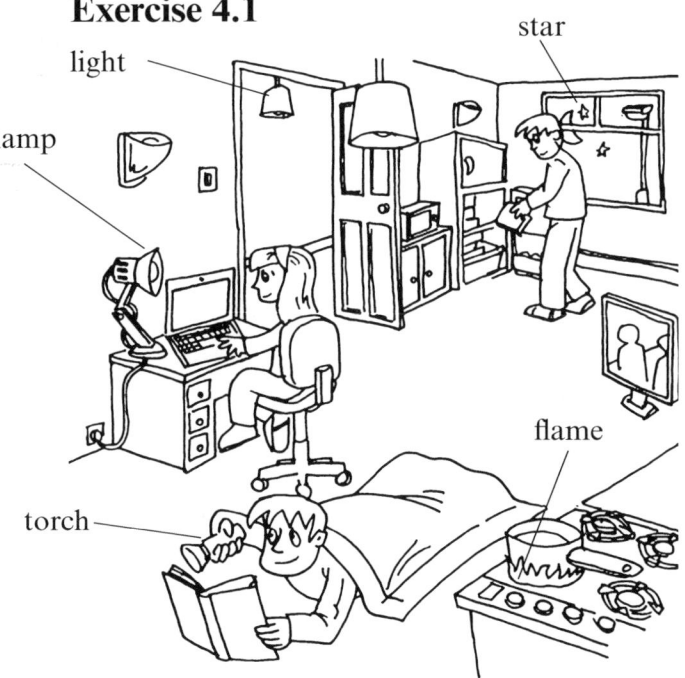

Answers to Worksheets

Worksheet 4.1a

Learners' predictions and results from testing a variety of objects in Activity 4.1, some of which were light sources and others which were not light sources.

Worksheet 4.1b

Light sources: stars, torch, table lamp, lit candle

Not light sources: flower, bike, coat, sandwich

Topic 4.2 Darkness

In this topic, learners explore darkness.

Learning objectives

- Know that darkness is the absence of light.
- Collect evidence by making observations when trying to answer a science question.
- Use first-hand experience.
- Predict what will happen before deciding what to do.
- Make and record observations.
- Use a variety of ways to tell others what happened.
- Talk about predictions (orally and in text), the outcome and why this happened.
- Review and explain what happened.

Curriculum links

- This topic could be linked to literacy and language work using the stories suggested.
- If you have a curriculum that covers aspects of your own and other cultures, you could link to the concept of the 'Festival of Lights', which is a feature of many cultures and religions.

Ideas for the lesson

- Introduce the topic of darkness by reading a story about being scared of the dark. *Mog in the Dark* by Judith Kerr or *Can't You Sleep, Little Bear?* by Martin Waddell can both be used. *Can't You Sleep, Little Bear?* also allows for a discussion about light sources. *The Owl Who Was Afraid of the Dark* by Jill Tomlinson could also be used, but it is a longer book that could be read over several days.
- Talk with learners about when they have been out in the dark. Ask them how they felt and why they think some people are scared of the dark. Then ask them when it can be fun to be in the dark. Learners may suggest that getting to see the Moon and stars is fun.

Or they may say that they enjoy playing in the Dark Den or seeing how shadows change as they walk between streetlights. Learners may talk about night time celebrations that use fireworks, lanterns or bonfires; Picture 4.2 on the CD-ROM can be used to illustrate this. At this point, you could explore why certain cultures have a Festival of Lights – often this coincides with the end of the darkest time of the year.

- Ask learners to cover their eyes with their hands. Ask them to describe what they can see. Typical responses might include that it is a bit dark or that they can see light coming in the gaps. Explain that to make it completely dark we have to block out all the light. Discuss the picture on page 40 of the Learner's Book. Talk about how there is often some light in a bedroom at night – from street lights or from light sources such as digital alarm clocks or standby lights on electrical items.

- In Activity 4.2 learners make observations first-hand using a dark box. Demonstrate how to use a dark box then ask learners to predict what they will see before trying it themselves. (See *Notes on practical activities* section). Worksheet 4.2 supports this activity.

- Exercise 4.2 in the Activity Book asks learners to review and explain the dark box experiment in Activity 4.2.

- Ask learners to investigate the Dark Den from Topic 4.1. Send learners inside the Dark Den without any light sources. Ask them to find out whether it is completely dark. If they can see, ask them to try to find where the light is getting in. If the Dark Den is not completely dark, ask learners to make suggestions of how to improve it. They might suggest using thicker, darker or more layers of fabric. Or they may suggest making sure that there are no gaps by piling up some fabric around the base of the den. Some learners may observe that turning off the lights in the classroom might make the den darker.

Notes on practical activities

Activity 4.2

Each pair or group will need:
- a small cardboard box with a lid
- a small object to go in the box
- torch.

Before this activity, you will need to make some dark boxes. It is very simple. A cardboard box with a lid is needed – A4 paper boxes or shoe boxes are ideal. Stick black card over any gaps where light could get in. Use a craft knife to make a flap in the lid about 3 cm × 3 cm. Use a sharp point to make a tiny hole in the side. This hole needs to be small to prevent light getting in. A circular hole about 0.5 cm diameter works well – smaller than the diameter of a pencil. It is best if this viewing hole is at a similar height to the object being placed in the box. Place a toy or other object in the centre of the box. Secure the object in place, with glue or sticky tape, to stop it sliding away from the viewing hole as the box is moved around. Make several boxes and learners can work in groups on this activity.

When learners first look into the box through the viewing hole, the top flap should be closed. It should be too dark in the box for them to see the object. If there is still some light getting in, you will need to cover any gaps or use a smaller viewing hole. The second time, open the top flap to let in some light. Ask learners to look again. Now they should be able to see something. But it may still be hard to work out what the object is. To use the torch, encourage learners to work in pairs – one can shine the torch through the top flap, the other can look through the viewing hole. They should now be able to see the object fairly well.

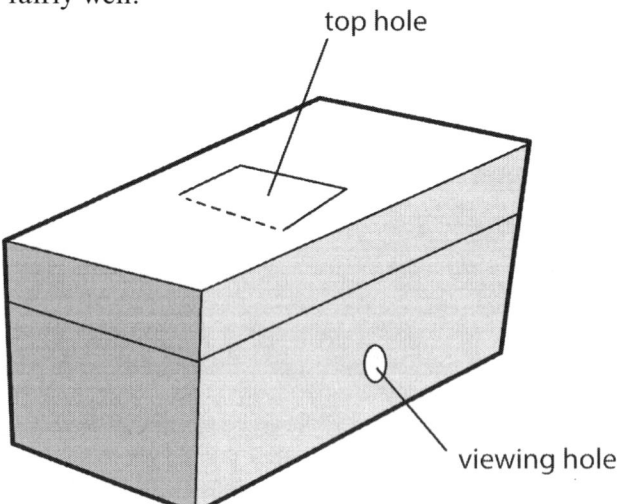

Ask learners to predict whether they will be able to see each time, before they collect evidence by making observations. Afterwards, compare the results with their predictions. Learners can record their observations using Worksheet 4.2 and use it to tell others what happened. Some learners may want to guess what object is in the box. This game should be avoided in this activity because learners need to focus on whether they can see or not, rather than what they can see. Learners can review and explain this activity using Exercise 4.2 in the Activity Book.

Internet and ICT

- Learners could use a camera with the flash turned off to take photographs in the Dark Den. This would show that cameras cannot see in the dark either.

- The website www.childrensuniversity. manchester.ac.uk/interactives/science/ brainandsenses/eye/ gives information about how the eye works. It would be suitable for higher achieving learners.

Assessment

- After Activity 4.2, ask learners to work in pairs and take turns to describe the stages of what they have just done. Choose pairs of learners to repeat their explanations to the whole class. This allows learners to develop the scientific enquiry skills of reviewing and explaining what happened.

Differentiation

- If any lower achieving learners have difficulty with the dark box activity, remove the lid of the box and place the box inside the Dark Den from Topic 4.1. Ask these learners to go inside the Dark Den with no light source at first. Then ask them to use a torch to identify the object inside the box.

- After Activity 4.2 ask higher achieving learners to observe how the pupil of the eye changes in different light conditions. They could use the Dark Den and the bright classroom to compare. They should be able to see that the pupil is larger when there is less light. Extend higher achieving learners further by asking them to find out more about how the eye works. They could use information from the website in the *Internet and ICT* section to help them.

 **Safety** Tell learners not to touch their eyes as this can cause infection or damage.

Common misunderstandings and misconceptions

- Darkness is a lack of light rather than a thing in itself. Some learners may think that you can make a room dark by adding darkness rather than by removing light. Experiences in the Dark Den using torches and other light sources should counter this.

- Many learners will say that they can see in the dark. Dark can mean 'not much light' and it can mean 'no light'. Talk about these two meanings with learners. Explain that if there is 'not much light' we can see but it might take our eyes a little while to adjust. But if there is 'no light' we cannot see.

- Some learners may think that eating carrots will help them to see in the dark.

Homework ideas

- Exercise 4.2 in the Activity Book.

Answers to Activity Book exercise

Exercise 4.2

It is too dark to see.

There is some light. It is hard to see.

It is light. She can see well.

Answers to Worksheet

Worksheet 4.2

The darkest shading used by the learners should be in the closed box. This should have no picture of an object as it would have been too dark to see.

The lightest shading used by the learners should be in the open box with the torch. This should also have a drawing of the object as seen.

The open box with no torch should have shading in between those of the boxes above. There may be a drawing of all or part of the object as seen.

Topic 4.3 Making shadows

In this topic, learners explore shadows.

Learning objectives

- Be able to identify shadows.
- Use first-hand experience.
- Talk about risks and how to avoid danger.
- Make and record observations.
- Identify simple patterns and associations.

Curriculum links

- This topic links to Topic 6.3, which looks at how the position of shadows changes throughout the day.
- Links could be made to literacy and language work using the stories suggested.

Ideas for the lesson

- Read learners a story about shadows, such as *The Man Who Sold his Shadow* by Peter Schlemiel or one of the stories on the internet (see *Internet and ICT* section below.) The story *Suddenly!* by Colin McNaughton shows many shadows in the pictures. Talk with learners about what they know about shadows. Ask learners to say when they see them and to talk about the shape of shadows.
- Talk about the picture on page 42 of the Learner's Book. Alternatively, you could use Picture 4.3 on the CD-ROM; this shows pictures of two interesting shadows, as well as a picture illustrating that an object can have more than one shadow if there is more than one light source.

- In Activity 4.3 learners are asked to draw around a shadow. On a sunny day, take the learners into the playground to make and draw around their shadows.
- In the playground, challenge learners to make a gap between themselves and their shadow – they can do this by jumping. Then ask them whether they can touch the head of their shadow – they can do this by crouching down or standing so their shadow falls on a wall. Worksheet 4.3a can be used after this activity to record their first-hand observations.
- Give learners a selection of small objects and torches. Objects could include erasers, small 3D shapes, model people and other small toys. In pairs, ask learners to put the object on paper and use the torch to make a shadow of the object. Ask them to draw around the shadow and look at the association between object and shadow. Learners could then use crayons or art pencils to shade in the shadows. Worksheet 4.3b can be used to record observations for this activity. If possible, darken the classroom by closing the blinds or putting dark paper over the windows.
- Exercise 4.3 in the Activity book asks learners to identify simple associations by matching objects to their shadows. It could be used with all learners or as support for lower achieving learners.

Notes on practical activities

Activity 4.3

Each pair or group will need:
- chalk

Begin by asking learners to identify the light source that creates outdoor day-time shadows.

Talk with learners about not looking directly at the Sun. Talk about the risks and how to avoid danger.

 Learners should be warned never to look directly at bright light sources, especially the Sun, as this can damage their eyes.

Ask learners to work in pairs – one learner can make a shadow; the other can draw around the shadow with chalk. They can then swap roles. Learners can make the shadows interesting by changing how they stand.

If you ask learners to mark where to stand with a cross, then other learners can try to make the same shadow, moving until their shadow fits the chalk line. Ask learners to observe their shadows carefully as they will have to draw them when they get back to class. To help learners understand the position of their shadows, ask them to point at the Sun with one hand and point at their shadow with the other. They should be able to identify the association that their shadow is in the opposite direction from the Sun.

Ask learners to find and mark other shadows such as those of trees, playground equipment and buildings.

Back in class, ask learners to record their observations by drawing a picture of themselves, the Sun and their shadow. Remind learners about the position of their shadow in relation to the Sun. Talk about how much detail their shadow should have. If possible, show learners photographs of shadows taken in the playground.

Internet and ICT

- There are stories about shadows at these websites: www.stuartstories.com/ stories/boyandshadow.html and www.bygosh.com/Features/072000/ shadow.htm.

- In the playground, learners could take digital photographs of their shadows. They can look at them back in class.

Assessment

- After Activity 4.3, ask learners to look at each other's drawings of shadows and say one thing they like and one thing that they could improve.

Differentiation

- In Activity 4.3, lower achieving learners may make more accurate observations if you ask them questions about their shadow whilst outside. Ask them to describe what their shadow looks like. Ask specific questions, such as whether their shadow has a nose or eyes, whether they can see the details of clothing and whether their shadow is joined to themselves.

- Ask higher achieving learners to predict what would happen if they tried to make the same shadow later in the day. These learners could test their predictions later on.

Note: because the Sun appears to move across the sky, the shadows will not fall in the same place later in the day. There is a full investigation into this in Unit 6.

Common misunderstandings and misconceptions

- Some learners may try to draw shadows with facial features and clothing details. Encourage them to look more carefully at real shadows and photographs.

Homework ideas

- Exercise 4.3 in the Activity Book.

Answers to Activity Book exercise

Exercise 4.3

Answers to Worksheets

Worksheet 4.3a

Learners draw their own shadows.

Worksheet 4.3b

Learners draw the shadows of different objects.

Topic 4.4 Shadow shapes

In this topic, learners make shadow puppets.

Learning objectives

- Be able to identify shadows.
- Use simple information sources.
- Identify simple patterns and associations.
- Review and explain what happened.
- Use first-hand experience.

Curriculum links

- There are links with English, story sequencing and Drama in this topic as learners have the opportunity to create and perform a short play using shadow puppets.

Ideas for the lesson

- On a sunny day, take the learners outside and ask them to work together to make shadow monsters with their bodies, arms and legs. Challenge them to make a shadow that has more than two arms, two legs and one head.

- Talk about the picture on page 44 of the Learner's Book. You could also refer to Picture 4.3 on the CD-ROM here.

- You could use Picture 4.4 on the CD-ROM to introduce the idea of shadow puppets.

- In Activity 4.4a learners are asked to make shadow puppets with their hands.

- Show learners a video of a shadow puppet play performance – see the website suggested in the *Internet and ICT* section below. Make and show learners a simple shadow puppet with cut out sections to let light through. Ask learners to explain why the shadow has both dark and light patches. Encourage learners to explore how the cut out sections in the puppet lead to light patches in the shadow by using the puppet and covering parts of it with their hands or coloured transparent plastic.

- Activity 4.4b asks learners to make their own shadow puppets.

- Learners could work in groups to create a short shadow puppet play using their shadow puppets. The play could follow the plot of a familiar story. Groups of learners can then perform their play to others either using the shadow puppet screen or using an overhead or data projector.

- Learners can use Worksheet 4.4 to predict and investigate the shadows of different objects. Ask the learners to observe the shape of the object carefully. Then ask them to discuss their prediction of the shadow of each object before recording their prediction on the worksheet. Ask learners to suggest ways that they could investigate the actual shadows of the objects. They might suggest taking the objects outside if it is sunny. Or they might suggest using a torch, projector or other light source. They can record their

observations of the actual shadows on the worksheet and then discuss whether the results matched their predictions. If possible, darken the classroom by closing the blinds or putting dark paper over the windows.

- In Exercise 4.4 in the Activity Book, learners think about the association between an object and its shape. They are asked to predict and draw the shadow of simple objects.

Notes on practical activities

Activity 4.4a

Each pair or group will need:
- a light source
- a screen.

Encourage learners to practise making the hand shapes shown in the Learner's Book before making the shadows. The shadows could be made using an overhead projector, a data projector or outside in the sunshine. Alternatively, a shadow puppet screen can be made by fixing white cotton fabric or thin paper into a frame made of wood or strong card. This can then be lit from behind. The learner making the shadow stands between the light source and the screen and the audience watch from in front of the screen. Allow learners to try further shadow hand puppet shapes using simple information sources (see the *Internet and ICT* section below).

Ask learners to observe the simple associations between their shadow hand puppet shapes and the shadows on the screen. If more than one learner is making shapes on the screen, can they identify which shadow belongs to which hand shape?

Activity 4.4b

Each pair or group will need:
- opaque card
- scissors
- glue
- a light source
- a screen.

Learners can make shadow puppets from opaque card. They could use the templates on Resource Sheet 4.4.

Ask learners to demonstrate their shadow puppet to others. As for Activity 4.4a, the learner with the puppet stands between the light source and the screen and the puppet throws a shadow onto the screen. Encourage learners to talk about the shape of the shadow and how any light patches within the shadow are made. This allows them to demonstrate the scientific enquiry skills of identifying simple patterns and associations and reviewing and explaining what happened.

Internet and ICT

- There are more shadow hand puppet shapes here: www.kellys.com/ashley/shadow.html.
- The following website includes more templates for making shadow puppets from card: home.comcast.net/~pizzicatopuppets/myoshadow.html.
- Show learners the 'Hand Shadow' video here: www.saxton.com.au/raymond-crowe/#videos.
- This video shows shadow puppets being made and used in a show: www.bbc.co.uk/learningzone/clips/how-shadows-are-made-shadow-puppets/2175.html.

Assessment

- Ask learners to assess each other's work from Worksheet 4.4 by comparing their predictions with the shadows observed. Challenge learners to describe any differences between the predictions and results and to say why the difference happened.

Differentiation

- Lower achieving learners may find it difficult to draw the shadows of more complicated shapes. Support them by giving them a selection of simpler shapes to investigate.
- In Activity 4.4b, learners can change the size of the shadow by moving the puppet closer or further away from the screen. Challenge higher achieving learners by asking them to demonstrate this. Ask them to explain to others about how to make a large or small shadow.

Common misunderstandings and misconceptions

- Some learners may try to draw shadows with facial features and clothing details. Encourage them to look more carefully at real shadows and photographs.

Homework ideas

- Exercise 4.4 in the Activity Book.

Answers to Activity Book exercise

Exercise 4.4

Answers to Worksheet

Worksheet 4.4

Learners draw predicted and observed shadow shapes for a ruler, paper clip, book, comb and tracing paper.

Topic 4.5 Check your progress

Learning objectives

- Review the learning for this unit.

Ideas for the lesson

- Learners can be asked to answer the questions on the 'Check your progress' pages of the Learner's Book (pages 46–47). These questions cover topics from the whole unit. Some answers are ambiguous, which will lead to discussion that will help to assess learners' understanding of this unit.

Answers to Learners' Book questions

1   The candle and Sun (C and D) are light sources, the others are not. Some learners may say that the Moon and mirror are light sources, but these just reflect light from other sources.

2   a   Drisha cannot find the ball because it is too dark. There is not enough light for her to see the ball.
    b   She could use a torch or another portable light source to help her find the ball.

3   The shadow of the girl has details that shadows do not have: the stripes on the dress and facial features. The shadow should be plain grey with no features.
    The shadow of the tree is pointed the wrong way. It should be pointing away from the Sun.
    The shadow of the bicycle should have light parts where light can get through the holes in the frame of the bicycle.

4   He should shine a light source behind the puppet and put a screen in front of the puppet.

Resource sheet 4.1a

Night-time light sources

Cut out these light sources to make a night-time picture.

Vocabulary cards: Part 1

light sources	
not light sources	
light	
reflect	
Moon	
Sun	

Resource sheet 4.1b

Vocabulary cards: Part 2

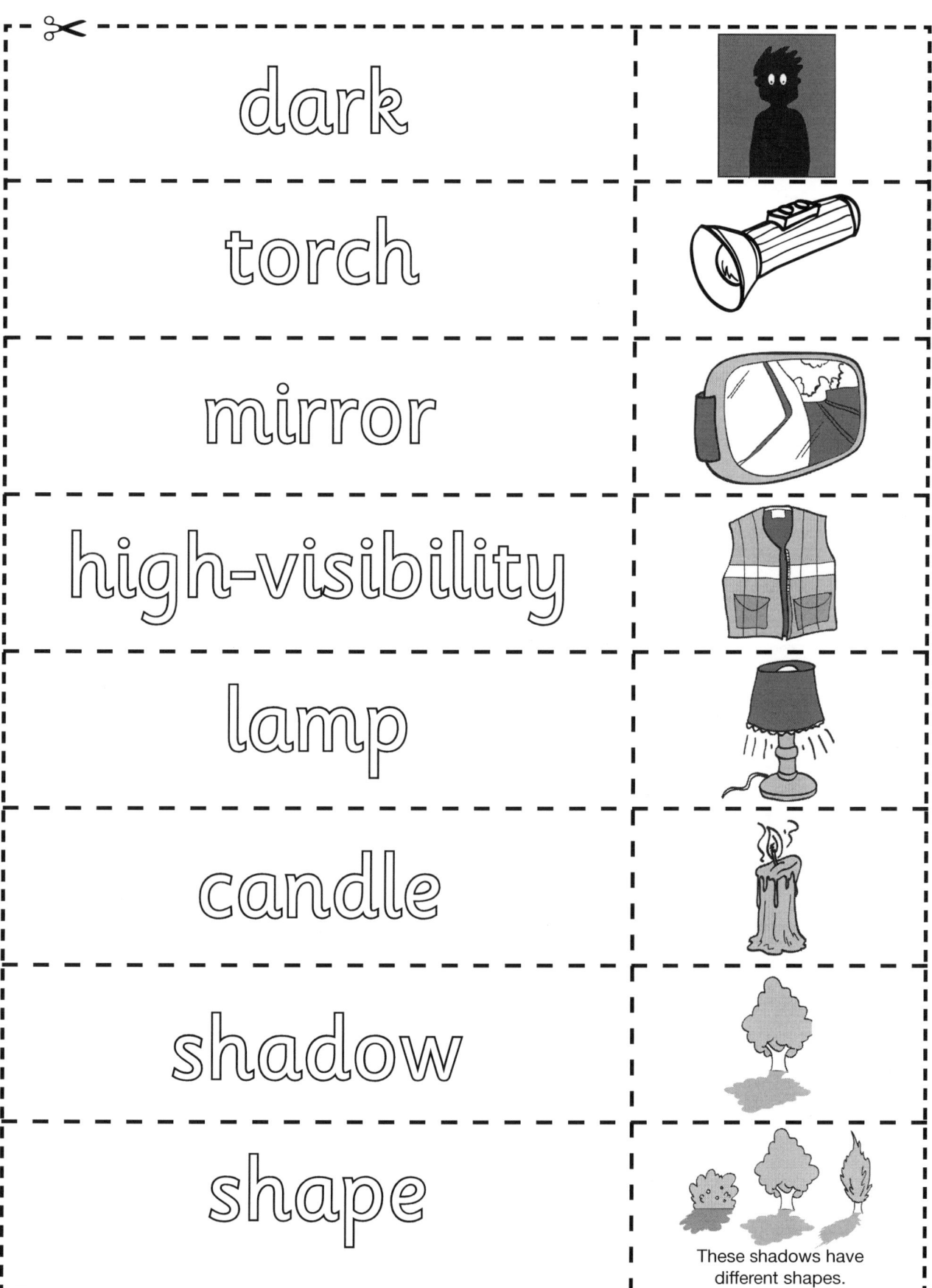

dark

torch

mirror

high-visibility

lamp

candle

shadow

shape

These shadows have different shapes.

Shadow puppets: Part 1

Cut out these shapes to make shadow puppets.

Cambridge Primary Science 2

Shadow puppets: Part 2

Cut out these shapes to make shadow puppets.

Worksheet 4.1a

Is it a light source?

Name: _____ Date: _____

Which objects make light?

Draw the objects in the correct box.

Predict What do you think?	**Observe** What did you find out?
light sources	light sources
not light sources	not light sources

Compare your observations and predictions.

What have you learnt?

Cambridge Primary Science 2

Worksheet 4.1b

Sorting light sources

Name: _____ Date: _____

Cut out the pictures and sort them. Is each one a light source or not?

light sources 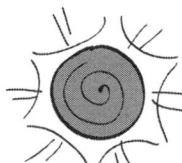	not light sources 

Can you see in the dark?

Name: _____ Date: _____

What did it look like in the box?

Cut and stick the squares to show how dark it was.

Then draw on the square what you saw in each box.

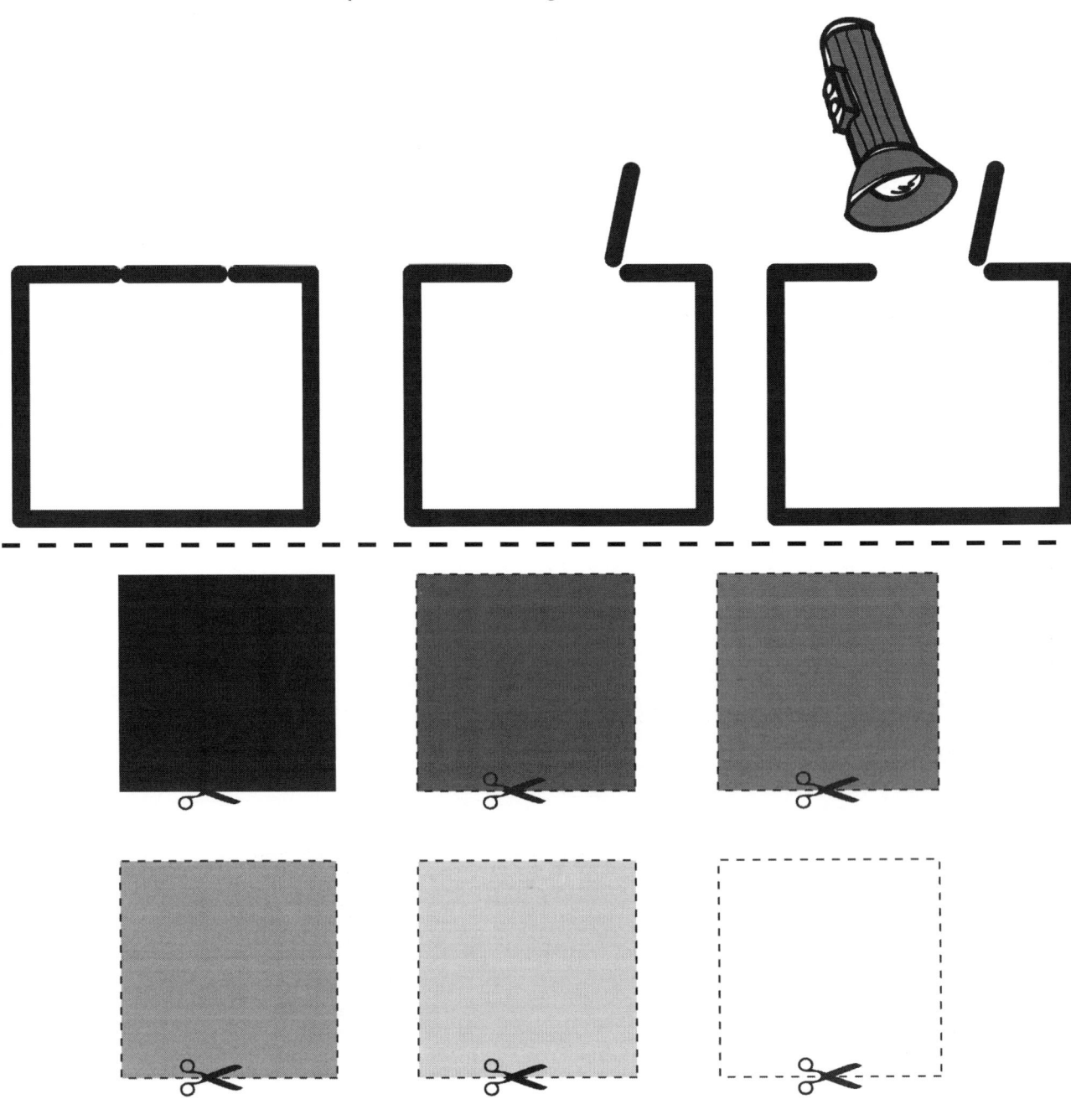

Worksheet 4.3a

Draw yourself and your shadow

Name: _____ Date: _____

Go outside.

Make a shape. Look carefully at your shadow.

Draw it here.

Tell your friends about your shadow.

Exploring shadows

Name: _____ Date: _____

Draw around the shadows of some objects.

Put object here X	Put object here X
Put object here X	Put object here X

Cambridge Primary Science 2

Worksheet 4.4

Look at the shadows of different objects

Name: _____ Date: _____

Draw what you think the shadows will look like.

Then collect the objects and find out.

Object	Prediction	Shadow
ruler		
paper clip		
book		
comb		
trac pap.		

Unit 5

Teaching ideas

Background knowledge

Electricity is caused by tiny, negatively charged particles called electrons. Electrons are one of the three particles that make up all atoms and so they are present in every substance. In metals and other conductors the electrons can move around. In a circuit they flow inside the metal of the wires, making the components work. The electrons in a circuit flow from the negative terminal of the cell to the positive terminal. (However, the conventional current in a circuit is from positive to negative. This convention was chosen during the discovery of electricity when scientists presumed that electrons had a positive charge. This was a wrong assumption!)

An electrical cell, or battery, provides a force that pushes the electrons round the circuit. The voltage of a cell determines how strongly it pushes the electrons around the circuit. The bigger the voltage, the bigger the push. This explains why it is safe to investigate circuits using small voltages, but it is not safe to investigate circuits with a mains supply of 220–240 V. 220 V is enough to push electricity through a human body, 3 V is not.

Buzzers and light emitting diodes (LEDs) only work in a circuit when they are connected the correct way round. To connect them correctly, the red wire must be connected to the positive terminal of the cell, usually labcllcd ' I ', and the black wire to the negative terminal, sometimes labelled '−', but also sometimes unlabelled.. Normal light bulbs will work either way around, as will a motor. However, how the motor is connected will determine which way it spins.

An electrical cell is a device that produces electricity from chemicals. Strictly speaking, the term 'battery' refers to when two or more of these cells are connected together. However, in common language, 'battery' is often used to describe a single sealed cell such as an AAA, AA, C or D battery.

Cells supply d.c. electricity. This stands for 'direct current' and means that the electrons are all moving in the same direction around the circuit from one end of the cell to the other. Mains circuits are a.c. or 'alternating current'. Here, the electrons move one way along the wire and then the other. They vibrate backwards and forwards.

Static electricity is a build-up of charge (positive or negative) in a material. An object such as a balloon can become statically charged when it is rubbed with fabric. The rubbing causes some of the electrons from the fabric to move onto the balloon. This causes the balloon to become negatively charged and the fabric to become positively charged. The balloon is then attracted to the fabric or any other surface that is more positively charged than itself, such as a wall. Lightning is caused by static electricity. During a storm, particles within clouds move around and the static charge builds up. When it is large enough, a huge spark jumps towards an uncharged body, such as the ground. Static electricity is not covered in this unit, but learners may ask questions about phenomena such as lightning which are caused by static electricity.

Connecting a single wire directly from one terminal of a cell to the other creates a 'short circuit' where the electricity flows very quickly along the wire and through the cell, making them both hot. If a short circuit is left connected for some time, the cell can begin to smoke, leak or even burst. Learners are unlikely to create a short circuit as they are trying to construct larger circuits using other components. Rechargeable cells should not be used as they can become extremely hot if short circuited.

Learners will be taught about how switches work and more about what electricity is at Stage 4.

Unit overview

Topic	Number of lessons	Outline of lesson content	Resources in Learner's Book	Resources in Activity Book	Resources in Teacher's Resource
5.1 Electricity around us	1–2	Learners identify electrical items and the difference between mains electricity and electrical cells.	Activity 5.1 Electricity around us SE	Exercise 5.1 SE Su Ex	Worksheet 5.1 SE L
5.2 Staying safe	1	Learners find out how to stay safe with mains electricity.	Activity 5.2 Electrical safety SE Su Ex	Exercise 5.2 SE	Worksheet 5.2 SE Resource sheet 5.2 L Su
5.3 Making a circuit	1–2	Learners build some simple circuits with bulbs.	Activity 5.3 Can you make a bulb light up? SE	Exercise 5.3 SE L Su	Worksheet 5.3a SE L Worksheet 5.3b SE Su Worksheet 5.3c SE L Su Worksheet 5.3d SE Ex Resource sheet 5.3 Su
5.4 Using motors and buzzers	1–2	Learners build circuits with motors and buzzers.	Activity 5.4a Making a fan SE Ex Activity 5.4b, Using a buzzer SE	Exercise 5.4 L Su	Worksheet 5.4a SE L Su Worksheet 5.4b SE Resource sheet 5.4
5.5 Switches	1	Learners use switches in circuits.	Activity 5.5 Switch it on, switch it off SE L Su	Exercise 5.5 SE L Su	Worksheet 5.5 SE L Su
5.6 Check your progress			Questions 1 L , 2 L , 3 SE , 4 SE		

Ex Extension   L Language   SE Scientific enquiry   Su Supplementary

Resources

- cells (batteries)
- cell holders
- bulbs
- bulb holders
- wires
- masking tape
- card
- scissors
- sticky tack
- motors
- buzzers
- a simple kit or home-made electric motor
- cameras (optional)
- switches
- cardboard boxes and tubes
- construction kits

The larger C or D sized cells are easier for learners to handle. They also last longer than the smaller AA or AAA cells. Cells can be used singly or in pairs using cell holders.

Bulbs are marked with a voltage rating. This is the voltage at which they will shine brightly. If you are using single 1.5 V cells then 3 V bulbs are best. If you are using a cell of 3 V then a 4.5 V bulb is best. Using a bulb with a slightly higher voltage rating than the cells helps to protect the bulb if the learners connect more than one cell.

Motors and buzzers have similar voltage ratings to bulbs. However, they are less easily damaged so using the same voltage as the cells is recommended.

Single pole switches should be used because these have only two terminals. The best switches are knife switches, or other types where learners can see what is happening inside the switch.

Connecting wires are available which have metal crocodile clips at each end. These make building a circuit more manageable. However, you do need to check these because bad connections between the wire and the metal clips can occur.

Topic 5.1 Electricity around us

In this topic, learners look at how we use electricity. They find out the difference between mains electricity and cells. They also discover that electricity can make things move, make sound and light, and make things hot or cold.

Learning objectives

- Collect evidence by making observations when trying to answer a science question.
- Use simple information sources.
- Use first-hand experience.
- Make and record observations.

Curriculum links

- This topic could be linked to history. Learners could research how practical tasks around the home were done before electrical appliances were invented.
- The research activity in this topic has strong links with English.

Ideas for the lesson

- Before starting this topic, talk with learners about what they already know about electricity. Show learners the large picture on page 48 of the Learner's Book to help with the discussion. Some learners might be able to describe appliances that use electricity at home or at school. Some will know that many portable items use cells. Many will know that electricity can be dangerous. Some learners may be aware that mains electricity is made in power stations and transported by power lines. Others may talk about lightning or other types of static electricity. Ask learners to draw a picture showing what they know about electricity. They could include things that use electricity and electrical safety. While they do this, ask groups of learners to explain their pictures and to talk about what they know.
- Talk briefly with learners about keeping safe with mains electricity. Learners should never touch mains electrical equipment unless an adult tells them it is safe to do so. Electrical safety will be covered in more detail in Topic 5.2.
- Ask learners what they know about where mains electricity comes from. Look at the photograph of the power station in the Learner's Book on page 49 and ask learners to look at the power lines. Ask if they have seen overhead power lines bringing electricity to homes and other buildings. **Note:** Some areas have underground electricity cables but overhead telephone wires. Power lines tend to be thicker and have ribbed insulators where they are connected to the supporting poles. Phone lines are thinner and do not need insulators where they are connected to the poles.

- Use the Learner's Book to identify the difference between appliances that use mains electricity and those that use cells. Cell-powered items need less power and are often portable. Picture 5.1 on the CD-ROM can also be used here.

- Activity 5.1 is designed to help learners to answer the question 'What is electricity used for?' Take learners on a walk around the school. Ask them to collect evidence by identifying things that use electricity and things that do not. Back in class, ask learners to record their observations. They should make a list of electrical items they have seen. Help them to sort the list into those that use cells and those that use mains electricity. Learners can then draw and label some examples under relevant headings.

- Ask learners to use simple information sources such as non-fiction books to find out some new facts about electricity. Learners can use Exercise 5.1 in the Activity Book.

- Demonstrate how to open a torch and remove the cells. Ask learners to observe the cells carefully to notice that the two ends look different. Ask them to look closely to find a positive (+) and a negative (–) sign at the ends. (Some cells have only one end labelled.) Explain to learners that things will usually not work if the cells are the wrong way round. Demonstrate that there is often a picture to show which way round the cells should be. Give learners a selection of cell-powered items and ask them to remove the cells carefully. Swap their items. Then ask learners to find the right-sized cells for their item and to insert the cells correctly to make it work. Some items have cell covers that can be difficult to remove, or are screwed down. You will need to remove these before this activity.

- Talk with learners about the advantages and disadvantages of using cells. Help learners to identify that they are portable but that they 'go flat' – run out of power. Talk with learners about rechargeable batteries and explain that it is very dangerous to try to recharge normal cells as they can catch fire.

- Learners can use Worksheet 5.1 to sort pictures of household items into those that use electricity and those that do not.

Internet and ICT

- Learners will enjoy this interactive site about where electricity comes from: www.switchedonkids.org.uk/where_does.html.

Assessment

- Ask learners (in pairs) to tell each other their favourite mains-powered item and cell-powered item. Learners should explain their choices to each other. Ask learners to check that their partner has chosen one of each. Make sure that learners listen well by explaining that you will choose some learners to tell the class about their partner's choices.

Differentiation

- Lower achieving learners can research things that use electricity for Exercise 5.1.

- Higher achieving learners can research a wider range of electrical facts.

- For both sets of learners, provide them with books at a suitable reading level.

Common misunderstandings and misconceptions

- Some learners may think that bigger cells are more powerful. Look at different-sized cells to find the voltage label. AAA, AA, C, D and many button cells are all 1.5 V – the electrical push from these cells is the same. The difference is that larger cells have more energy so can last longer when doing the same task as a smaller cell.

- Some learners may think that all household items that move use electricity. If possible, demonstrate clockwork items to learners and show them the mechanism inside. Some learners will think that taps use electricity to make the water come out. If possible, show learners how a tap is connected by looking under a sink. Explain that the water is being pushed in the pipe. Turning the tap just opens a hole that lets the water run out.

- Some learners may think that mobile phones use mains electricity because they have seen them plugged in when charging. Explain that some special cells can be re-charged, using mains electricity, when they go flat.

Homework ideas

- Exercise 5.1 in the Activity book can be completed at home.

- Worksheet 5.1 is a suitable homework activity.

Answers to Activity Book exercise

Exercise 5.1

The six answers will depend on what the learners find in their books on electricity. Any sensible suggestions for devices that use electricity, correctly named, should be marked as correct.

Answers to Worksheet

Worksheet 5.1

Uses electricity	lamp, TV, torch, kettle, food mixer, fridge, mobile phone, MP3 player
Does not use electricity	pencil, stapler, toy car, scissors, can opener, toothbrush (not electric), glasses, tap

Topic 5.2 Staying safe

In this topic, learners find out about some of the dangers of mains electricity and how to avoid them.

Learning objectives

- Use simple information sources.
- Talk about risks and how to avoid danger.
- Use a variety of ways to tell others what happened.

Curriculum links

- This topic has links to personal, health and social education because learners find out how to keep safe with mains electricity.
- When learners carry out research, there are links to literacy.

Ideas for the lesson

- Explain to learners that mains electricity is very powerful and has to be used carefully. Learners should never touch mains electrical equipment unless an adult tells them it is safe to do so. Talk with learners about electrical safety and show them the pictures on pages 50 and 51 of the Learner's Book. Ask them to explain what they know about the dangers of electricity and water. Explain that mains electricity is powerful enough to flow through water (electricity from cells cannot do this unless the water is very salty).

- Show learners Picture 5.2 on the CD-ROM. This shows parts of the electrical supply outdoors. Talk with learners about staying away from electrical substations and power lines.

- Ask learners to use simple information sources to research how to stay safe with mains electricity. They could use the Learner's Book and other non-fiction sources, as well as websites such as those suggested in the *Internet and ICT* section. Activity 5.2 in the Learner's Book asks learners to make a poster to tell others how to stay safe with mains electricity. Learners will need to think about how to present information for a particular audience. You might ask them whether it would be sensible to present the information using many words, for example, or whether pictures would be better.

- Explain to learners that they are going to use cells to investigate circuits in this unit, and that this *will be safe*. Make it clear that it is not safe to investigate mains electricity.

- Learners can use Exercise 5.2 in the Activity Book to identify electrical dangers in the home.

- Learners can use Worksheet 5.2 to identify electrical dangers in a bathroom.

Internet and ICT

- Learners will enjoy this interactive site about electrical safety in the home: www.switchedonkids.org.uk/electrical-safety-in-your-home.

- These electrical safety websites are also suitable for learners: www.alliantenergykids.com/FunandGames/OnlineGames/007005; www.alliantenergykids.com/FunandGames/OnlineGames/007006; www.juniorcitizen.org.uk/kids/electricalsafety/electricalsafety.php.

- In these online games, learners can enter their name, class and school so they can print a certificate – indoor safety: www.auroraenergy.com.au/About/Safety/Safety-education/Sparky-s-electrical-safety-games/Sparky; outdoor safety: www.auroraenergy.com.au/About/Safety/Safety-education/Sparky-s-electrical-safety-games/Sparky-outside.

- Show learners this video about the danger of mains electricity: www.bbc.co.uk/learningzone/clips/mains-power-and-the-danger-of-electricity/2195.html.

Assessment

- Ask learners to work in small groups to make up and act out a short scene demonstrating how to stay safe around electricity. Encourage learners not to act out getting an electric shock, by explaining that the performance should end with one learner stopping another and explaining why what they are doing is dangerous. If learners perform their scene in silence, then other learners can try to guess the safety scenario.

Differentiation

- Lower achieving learners could make simple posters for younger children in the school in Activity 5.2. Support this group of learners by making a class display of the vocabulary for this unit. You could make use of Resource sheet 5.2 for this.

- You could ask higher achieving learners to design electrical safety posters for use around school or at home in Activity 5.2.

Common misunderstandings and misconceptions

- Many learners will think that they can get an electric shock from a cell or battery. A 1.5 V cell or 3 V battery will not give a person a shock. Sometimes a learner may catch their finger on a wire or motor terminal and may think they have been given a shock. Demonstrate to learners that touching both ends of a 1.5 V cell does not give a shock.

Homework ideas

- Exercise 5.2 in the Activity book could be completed at home.
- Worksheet 5.2 is a suitable homework activity.

Answers to Activity Book exercise

Exercise 5.2

Answers to Worksheet

Worksheet 5.2

These items should be coloured in red: hair dryer, wall light switch (or the wet hands), mains extension lead (or the puddle), radio.

Topic 5.3 Making a circuit

In this topic, learners are introduced to and build basic circuits.

Learning objectives

- Recognise the components of simple circuits involving cells (batteries).
- Collect evidence by making observations when trying to answer a science question.
- Use first-hand experience.
- Use simple information sources.
- Predict what will happen before deciding what to do.
- Talk about risks and how to avoid danger.
- Make and record observations.
- Use a variety of ways to tell others what happened.

Curriculum links

- This topic has links to design and technology, where learners might construct a working torch or model light house.

Ideas for the lesson

- Use the pictures on page 52 of the Learner's Book to introduce the learners to the components used in simple circuits. Then ask learners to complete Activity 5.3 where they are asked to work out how to build a simple circuit. The Learner's Book shows a diagram of the working circuit required, which you can point out to learners if they need help. (See *Notes on practical activities* section.) Worksheet 5.3a supports this activity.

- Look at the picture of the working circuit on page 53 of the Learner's Book. Explain to the learners that it is important for the circuit to make a single complete loop. Then ask them to use their fingers to trace the loop of the circuit in the picture, starting at the cell. Explain that the electricity has to be able to move around the circuit from one end of the cell, along the wires, through all the components and back to the cell.

- Use masking tape to mark out a large rectangular circuit on the floor. Explain to the learners that these strips of masking tape represent the metal in the wires and that they are going to act out being electricity. Ask them to stand in a queue along the wires. Choose one learner to act as the cell. Explain that the cell pushes the electricity to make it move around the circuit. Ask this 'cell' to stand on one side of the circuit and give each learner a gentle tap on the back as they shuffle past. Ask the 'cell' to say 'push' each time they tap a learner. Tell learners they should only shuffle around the circuit as long as they can hear the cell repeating 'push'. Choose one other learner to act as the bulb and stand on the opposite side of the circuit to the cell. As long as the electricity is moving, the 'bulb' can hold their hands in the air and smile to show that the bulb is on. If the electricity stops, the 'bulb' should drop their arms and look sad. Take care here with any cultural sensitivity around learners tapping each other.

- Use the same 'circuit' marked out with masking tape mentioned in the activity above. Make a small gap in the masking tape circuit on the floor. Explain to learners that they are not allowed to step over the gap so they have to stop at it. Ask learners to explain that none of them can move around the circuit because they cannot move across the gap. Learners will be able to see that electricity cannot flow in an incomplete circuit. This is a good model of what actually happens in an electric circuit. The learners are being the electrons, the tiny particles inside the metal wires. When a cell is connected to a circuit, the voltage of the cell pushes the electrons around inside the metal, very much like the learners in their queue. The model could be extended by labelling the cell with a positive and negative. This should be done so that the electrons are leaving from the negative side of the cell and returning to the positive. (See *Background knowledge* section.)

- Explain to learners that mains electricity is dangerous because the 'push' is so strong that it can move through water and even through people. This is why people can get electric shocks.

- Learners could make the different circuits in Worksheet 5.3b. (See *Notes on practical activities* section.) Worksheets 5.3c and 5.3d can be used to record this activity.

- When learners have been taught how to build a basic circuit, teach them how to check for faults with the circuit equipment. Talk with learners about what to do if they build a correct circuit but it does not work. Faults are caused by bad connections in the wires, by bulbs that are broken, or by flat batteries. Demonstrate a correct, but faulty, circuit and show learners how to check one part of the circuit at a time. Show them how to replace each wire, the bulb and the cell, one at a time until the circuit works. Ask learners to put any parts they think might be faulty to one side so they can be tested later.

- Exercise 5.3 in the Activity Book asks learners to identify working circuits, recording observations from their earlier work to tell others what happened.

Notes on practical activities

Activity 5.3 Can you make a bulb light up?

Each pair or group will need:
- a cell (battery)
- a cell holder
- a bulb
- a bulb holder
- two or more wires

Remind learners that circuits with batteries are safe to investigate, mains electricity is not. Learners should never touch mains electrical equipment unless an adult tells them it is safe to do so.

Challenge learners to work out how to build a simple circuit that lights a bulb. Make it clear to learners that you expect them to use trial and error to solve this problem. Explain that mistakes are actually useful; they are part of the learning process. Mistakes will teach them what does not work. If possible, allow learners to choose their own equipment but ask them to use the minimum number of wires that they think they need. Encourage learners to make predictions by telling their partners what they think they need to do and why. Encourage learners to investigate reversing the battery connections.

Learners can use Worksheet 5.3a to draw the working circuit they made and to review and explain what happened.

 Look out for learners short circuiting a battery with a single wire, as this will cause both the wire and battery to heat up.
Safety

Worksheet 5.3b What do these circuits do?

Each pair or group will need:
- a cell
- a cell holder
- a bulb
- a bulb holder
- two wires

Ask learners to predict what will happen in each circuit on the worksheet. They can record their predictions on the worksheet. Then ask learners to make each circuit and talk about what happens. In circuit D, learners are asked to remove the bulb from the holder. Encourage learners to observe the bulbs carefully to see the support wires and the filament inside. Resource sheet 5.3 has larger versions of the diagrams and can be used to support lower achieving learners.

Learners can use Worksheet 5.3c or 5.3d to draw their circuits and tell others what happened (see *Differentiation* section).

 Look out for learners short circuiting a battery with a single wire, as this will cause both the wire and battery to heat up.
Safety

Internet and ICT
- Learners can investigate circuits online here: www.bbc.co.uk/schools/scienceclips/ages/6_7/electricity.shtml.

Assessment
- In Worksheet 5.3b, ask groups of learners to show their circuits to another group. Ask the groups to check each other's circuits to make sure they match the pictures.

Differentiation
- Lower achieving learners could use Worksheet 5.3a as it provides support with language for recording Activity 5.3. This group of learners can use Resource sheet 5.3 in the activity on Worksheet 5.3b; ask these learners to build their circuits on top of the pictures of the circuits on the sheet. If some lower achieving learners are struggling to build the circuit, ask other learners to explain to how to do it – but not to make the circuit for them. To record their work in the activity on Worksheet 5.3b, learners can use Worksheet 5.3c which offers support for recording and language.
- Higher achieving learners can use Worksheet 5.3d to record their work in the activity on Worksheet 5.3b. This also challenges them to draw a circuit that uses two bulbs.

Common misunderstandings and misconceptions

- Some learners may think that electricity comes from a cell to the bulb and is used up as it is turned into light. These learners may expect the bulb to light up when only one wire is connected. Acting out electricity as described in the ideas for the lesson will help all learners understand how electricity works.

Homework ideas

- Exercise 5.3 in the Activity book could be completed at home.

Answers to Activity Book exercise

Exercise 5.3

Circuit 1: The bulb does light up.
Circuit 2: The bulb does not light up.
Circuit 3: The bulb does not light up.
Circuit 4: The bulb does light up.
Learners should colour in circuits 1 and 4.

Answers to Worksheets

Worksheet 5.3a

Learners draw and label the circuit they made. Any sensible, correctly labelled drawings should be marked as correct.

Worksheet 5.3b

Circuits A, B, C: No, they will not work.
Circuit D: Yes, it will work.

Worksheet 5.3c

Learners cut and stick components to create the circuits they made, and write explanations of what happened. Any sensible explanation that matches the circuit should be marked as correct.

Worksheet 5.3d

Learners draw the circuits they made, and write explanations of what happened. Any sensible explanation that matches the drawing should be marked as correct.

Topic 5.4 Using motors and buzzers

In this topic, learners are introduced to motors and buzzers.

Learning objectives

- Recognise the components of simple circuits involving cells (batteries).
- Collect evidence by making observations when trying to answer a science question.
- Predict what will happen before deciding what to do.
- Talk about risks and how to avoid danger.
- Make and record observations.
- Make comparisons.
- Identify simple patterns and associations.
- Talk about predictions (orally and in text), the outcome and why this happened.
- Review and explain what happened.

Curriculum links

- Links could be made with design and technology; learners could make vehicles powered by motors, and doorbells or simple alarms.

Ideas for the lesson

- Introduce the learners to motors and buzzers by showing them the components and asking them to predict what they do. Then look at the pictures on page 54 of the Learner's Book.
- Activity 5.4a asks learners to build a circuit using a motor. Activity 5.4b asks learners to build a circuit using a buzzer. (See *Notes on practical activities* section.) Worksheets 5.4a and 5.4b support these activities.
- Ask learners to search for electric motors inside electrical appliances in the classroom or take them on a hunt around your school. Ask them to think about other things from home that use motors. Electric motors are used in many items and can be found by listening for things that hum. Computers use motors to drive an internal fan and a hard disk, printers use motors to move the paper and the print heads, mobile phones use tiny unbalanced motors to make them vibrate. Learners may be able to identify washing machines, hairdryers, fans and electric screwdrivers or drills as things that spin and therefore use motors. Picture 5.4 on the CD-ROM can be used here.

- Talk with learners about electrical items in the home that use buzzers, for example alarm clocks and door bells. Identify any buzzers in the classroom such as the school bell. Simpler mobile phones often use a buzzer to make a loud ringtone but have a loudspeaker for the quieter conversation. The more complicated phone models, where there is a choice of ringtone, simply use the loudspeaker to play the ringtone and may not contain a buzzer at all.
- Demonstrate to learners a simple kit or home-made electric motor, so that they can see what happens inside. Learners will be amazed that even a single magnet can make a coil of wire spin. Remove the magnet from the motor to show that the coil will not move without the magnetic field. The simple explanation for how a motor works is that electricity flowing in a wire is magnetic.
- Exercise 5.4 in the Activity book asks learners to identify whether an item uses a motor or a buzzer.

Notes on practical activities

Activity 5.4a Making a fan

Each pair or group will need:
- one paper fan blade, one paper spiral and one paper circle with arrow all printed on card (you can use Resource sheet 5.4 to make these)
- scissors
- sticky tack
- a cell
- a cell holder
- two wires
- a motor

Remind learners that circuits with cells are safe to investigate, mains electricity is not. Learners should never touch mains electrical equipment unless an adult tells them it is safe to do so.

This activity builds on Activity 5.3. In this activity, the bulb in a circuit is replaced with a motor. Learners can cut out a fan blade from Resource sheet 5.4 and attach it to the motor using sticky tack. They should connect the cell and the motor with wires. Ask learners to collect evidence by observing the fan very carefully to answer the question 'Which way is it spinning?' Then ask them to predict what will happen if they swap the wires round. Some learners may predict that it will work as before – they may have noticed in Activity 5.3 that the bulb worked either way round. Others may predict that the motor will not work – they may have experience of electrical

items not working when the cells are the wrong way round. Other learners may predict that the motor will spin the other way round. Encourage learners to observe carefully to compare the direction of the motor. Learners may find it easier to identify the pattern by replacing the fan blades with the spirals or arrows on Resource sheet 5.4.

Ask learners to explain what they found out. This activity could be extended by asking learners to explain how motors and buzzers behave when the wires are swapped around. Learners can use Worksheet 5.4a or 5.4b to record their work (see *Differentiation* section).

Activity 5.4b Using a buzzer

Each pair or group will need:
- a cell
- a cell holder
- two wires
- a buzzer

Before starting this activity, explain to learners that it will be very noisy if every group has a buzzer making noise all the time. Ask them to say how they will be able to make their buzzer stop. Learner responses might include disconnecting the cell, removing the cell from the holder, or taking a wire off the buzzer. Remind learners about the activity where they acted out a circuit in Topic 5.3. They were the electricity moving along the metal in the wires. Explain that if there is a gap anywhere in the circuit, the electricity cannot move so the buzzer will stop. This introduces the idea of a switch, which is covered in the next topic.

Ask learners to build a circuit to make the buzzer work. Ask the learners to predict what will happen if they swap the wires around. Some learners may have already found this out if their circuit did not work to begin with. Encourage learners to identify the pattern of the buzzer which only works one way round in the circuit and compare this with the motor and bulb that work either way round. Ask learners to collect evidence by making observations then use Worksheet 5.4a or 5.4b to record their evidence.

Internet and ICT

- There are instructions on how to make a simple motor here: www.wikihow.com/Build-a-Simple-Electric-Motor.
- Learners could use cameras to take photographs of their working circuits. These could be made into a display or used in a presentation.

Assessment

- Ask learners to work in pairs and to talk about which electrical component they like best out of a bulb, a motor and a buzzer. Ask them to explain their choice by referring to either what the component does or how it is used. Ask pairs to feedback to the class.

Differentiation

- Lower achieving learners can be supported by giving them Worksheet 5.4a for Activities 5.4a and 5.4b. If some lower achieving learners are struggling to build the circuits, ask other learners to explain how to do it – but not to make the circuit for them.

- Higher achieving learners can be challenged in Activity 5.4a, by asking them to try to make the fan blow air by folding the blades of the fan slightly. This can be done by folding the shaded part of the blades upwards or downwards along the dotted line. Ask them to investigate what happens when the direction of the motor is reversed.

Common misunderstandings and misconceptions

- Many learners will expect the buzzer to work either way around in a circuit. This is a sensible prediction to make, given that both bulbs and motors do and learners are unlikely to have any experience of using buzzers. Some learners may think that wires are broken or that the cell is flat when they first put a buzzer in a circuit the wrong way round. This is easily corrected by asked them to turn the buzzer round.

Homework ideas

- Exercise 5.4 in the Activity Book could be completed at home.

Answers to Activity Book exercise

Exercise 5.4

Motor: washing machine, CD player, remote-controlled car, fan

Buzzer: alarm clock, door bell

Answers to Worksheets

Worksheet 5.4a

Learners cut and stick components to create the circuits they made, and write explanations of what happened. Any sensible explanation that matches the circuit should be marked as correct.

Worksheet 5.4b

Learners draw the circuits they made, and write explanations of what happened. Any sensible explanation that matches the drawing should be marked as correct.

Topic 5.5 Switches

In this topic, learners find out about switches and how they can be used to switch circuits on and off.

Learning objectives

- Know how a switch can be used to break a circuit.
- Use first-hand experience.
- Predict what will happen before deciding what to do.
- Talk about risks and how to avoid danger.
- Make and record observations.
- Review and explain what happened.

Curriculum links

- This topic can link with design and technology, where learners could use switches to control electrical models or even build their own switches.

Ideas for the lesson

- Build a whole class circuit. Give one learner a cell and one learner a bulb. Ask the other learners to stand in a circle, each holding a wire. Explain to the learners that they are going to try to make a large circuit to light the bulb. Ask learners to connect their wires with their neighbour's wires, with each learner holding a connection together with their fingers. The wires need to connect to the cell and the bulb too. This is quite difficult to do because there are many connections being held together by the learners.

If the learners work together well, they can make all the connections at once and the bulb will light up. The bulb will come on, but then go off when a learner moves and breaks a connection. Talk with learners about why the bulb was not always on. Encourage them to explain that if there is a gap in the circuit, the electricity cannot flow. This activity could also be done with lengths of metal foil instead of wires.

- Show learners the pictures of switches on page 56 of the Learner's Book and ask them to say what they think these switches do. The first two will switch on lights. The bottom left will switch on an electrical appliance and the bottom right will switch on an electric socket. Then show a real switch and explain that when it is off it makes a gap in a circuit; when it is on the circuit is complete.

- In Activity 5.5 learners make a circuit with a switch. (See *Notes on practical activities* section.) Worksheet 5.5 supports this activity.

- Show learners pictures of lighthouses, traffic lights, car indicators and other flashing lights. Picture 5.5 on the CD-ROM could be used here. Learners can build models of these from cardboard boxes and tubes. Show learners how to include circuits in their models that use switches to make the lights flash.

- Learners could work as a class to build a model town using construction kits. They could then add switched circuits with bulbs to control the lights inside buildings, circuits with buzzers to control doorbells, alarms and pedestrian crossing points, and circuits with motors to control model wind turbines.

- In Exercise 5.5 of the Activity Book, learners record their observations of circuits by showing which bulb is on in a circuit with a switch. They can also review and explain what happened with a short sentence.

Notes on practical activities

Activity 5.5 Switch it on, switch it off

Each pair or group will need:
- a switch
- a cell
- a cell holder
- three wires
- a bulb
- a bulb holder
- a buzzer or motor

Remind learners that circuits with cells are safe to investigate, mains electricity is not. Learners should never touch mains electrical equipment unless an adult tells them it is safe to do so. Remind learners that mains switches should never be touched with wet hands.

Ask learners to build a circuit where they can use a switch to control a bulb. Talk with learners about where a circuit like this would be useful, for example to control the headlights in a car, or a ceiling light at home. Learners can make predictions about what will happen if they use a buzzer or a motor in the circuit. Talk about these predictions, then give learners time to investigate before discussing whether their predictions were correct.

Learners can use Worksheet 5.5 to record their observations and to review and explain what happened.

Internet and ICT

- Learners could take digital photographs of switches, plugs, sockets and other mains equipment. These could then be labelled for a presentation or printed out and made into a class display.

Assessment

- Talk with groups of learners about how they are building their switched circuits. Ask learners to explain how their circuit works.

Differentiation

- Lower achieving learners may struggle to build the circuits. Ask other learners to explain how to do it – but not to make the circuits for them.

- Challenge higher achieving learners in Activity 5.5 by asking them to predict what would happen in a circuit with more than one switch. Then let them build the circuit to check their predictions.

Common misunderstandings and misconceptions

- Occasionally, learners may use two new wires to make a new loop in the circuit, connecting their switch only to the cell. This will cause a short circuit when the switch is in the 'on' position, so the bulb will not light up. When the switch is in the 'off' position the bulb will light up. Short circuits are dangerous as they will cause both the wire and cell to heat up.

- Some learners may connect their switch to the circuit incorrectly with both wires on one terminal. They will not be able to switch off the bulb.

Homework ideas

- Exercise 5.5 in the Activity Book can be completed at home.
- Ask learners to draw the electrical equipment they have at home and label any switches, wires or bulbs.

Answers to Activity Book exercise

Exercise 5.5

Circuit 1 should show wires connecting the components like this:

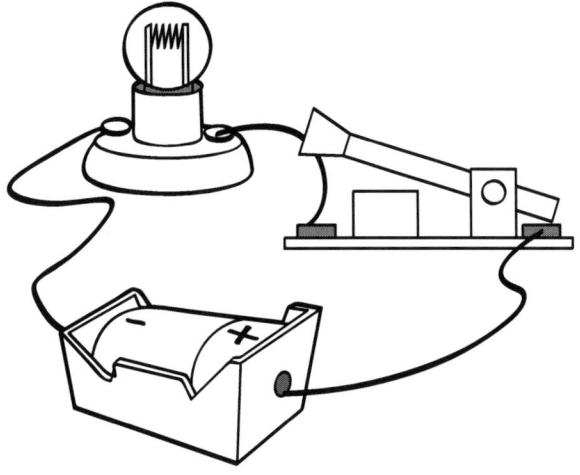

Learners should write 'This circuit is off'.

Circuit 2 should show wires connecting the components like this:

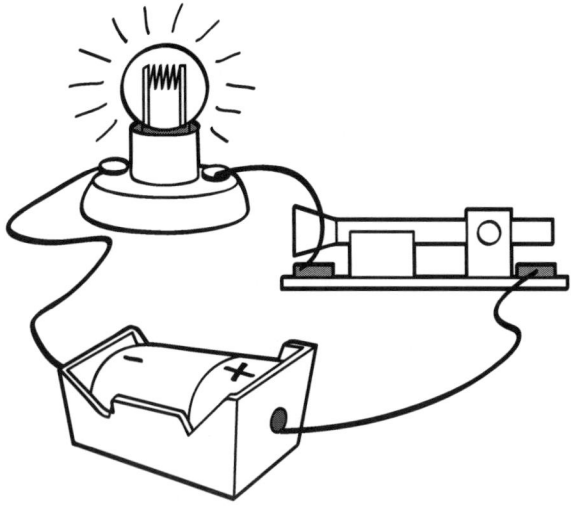

Learners should write 'This circuit is on'.

Answers to Worksheet

Worksheet 5.5

The switch was on. The bulb lit up. The motor turned. The buzzer buzzed.

The switch was off. The bulb did not light up. The motor did not turn. The buzzer did not buzz.

Topic 5.6 Check your progress

Learning objectives

- Review the learning for this unit.

Ideas for the lesson

- Learners can be asked to answer the questions on the 'Check your progress' pages of the Learner's Book. These questions cover topics from the whole unit. Some answers are ambiguous, which will lead to discussion that will help to assess learners' understanding of this unit.

Answers to Learner's Book questions

1   battery and cell
2   a bulb
    b motor
    c buzzer
    d switch
3   a No, this is not a complete circuit. The two wires both go to the same end of the cell.
    b No, this is not a complete circuit. There is only one wire to the motor.
    c Yes, this is a complete circuit with the positive side (red wire) of the buzzer connected to the positive terminal of the battery.
4   a Off. The switch is on but the bulb is only connected on one side.
    b Off. The circuit is correctly connected but the switch is off.

Vocabulary cards

mains electricity	
cell (battery)	
wire	
electric shock	
circuit	
bulb	
working circuit	
motor	
buzzer	
switch	

What do these circuits do?

A

B

C

D

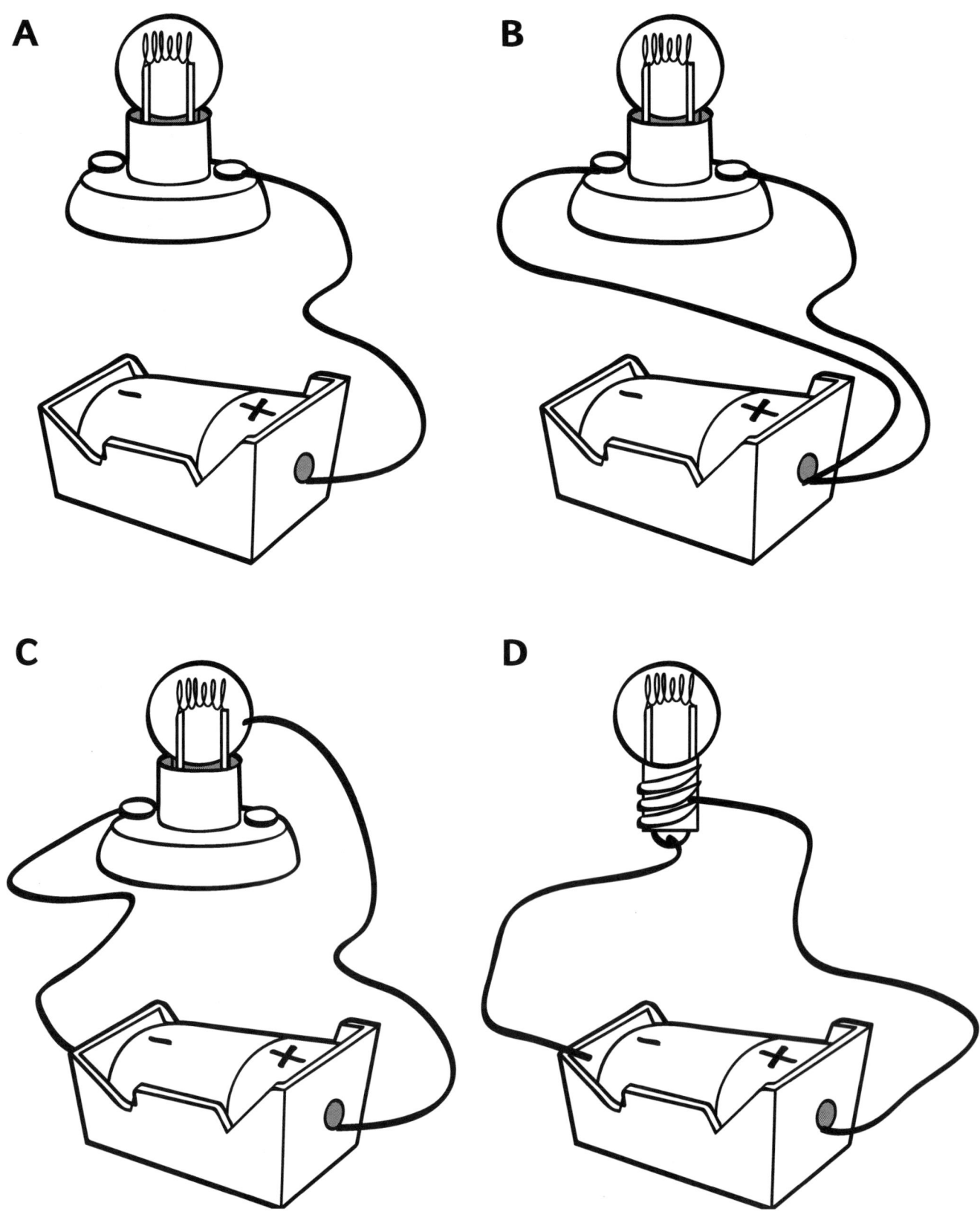

Making a fan

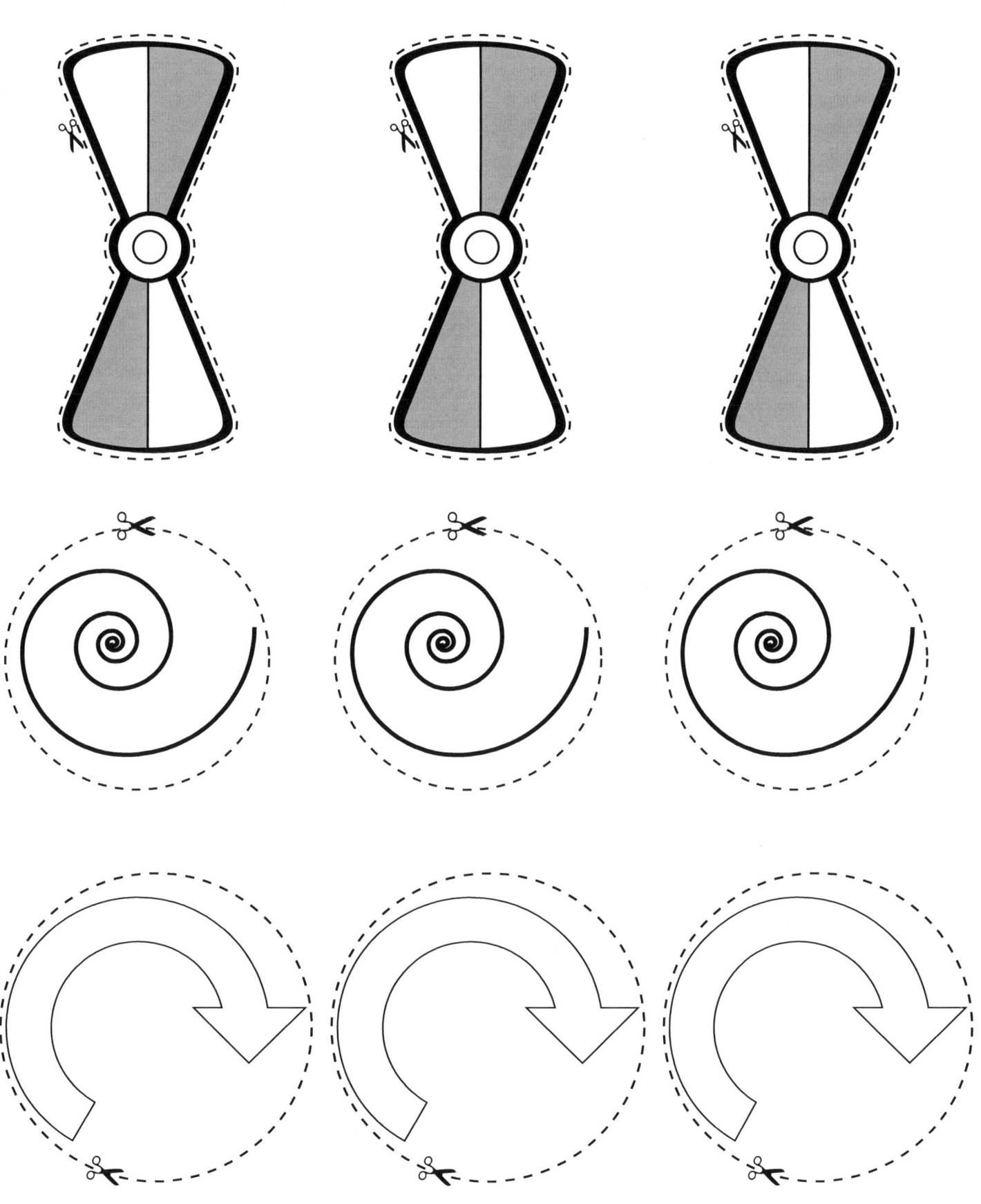

Worksheet 5.1

Electric or not?

Name: _____ Date: _____

Cut out the pictures.

Does each one use electricity? Stick them in the right box.

Uses electricity.	Does not use electricity.

Cambridge Primary Science 2

Worksheet 5.1

lamp	pencil	stapler	TV
toy car	scissors	torch	can opener
kettle	food mixer	toothbrush	mobile phone
glasses	tap	fridge	MP3 player

Worksheet 5.2

Be safe with mains electricity

Name: _____ Date: _____

Colour the dangers in red.
Colour the rest of the picture in other colours.

Cambridge Primary Science 2

Can you make a bulb light up?

Name: _____ Date: _____

Draw the circuit that you made.

Label these in your circuit

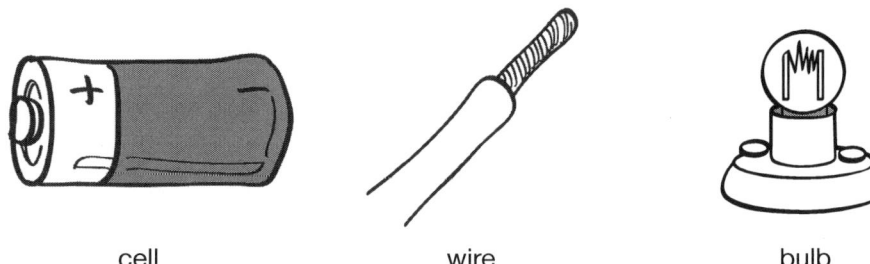

cell   wire   bulb

Worksheet 5.3b

What do these circuits do?

Name: _____ Date: _____

Do you think the bulb will light up in these circuits?

Circle Yes or No to show what you think will happen.

You will need:
- a cell
- a cell holder
- a bulb
- a bulb holder
- two wires

A

YES/NO

B

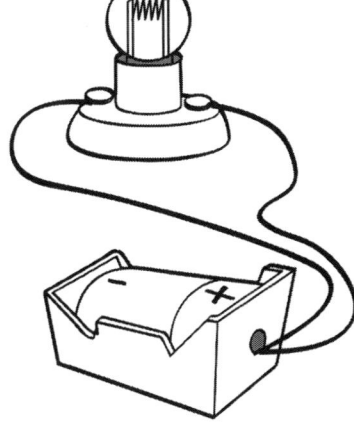

YES/NO

C

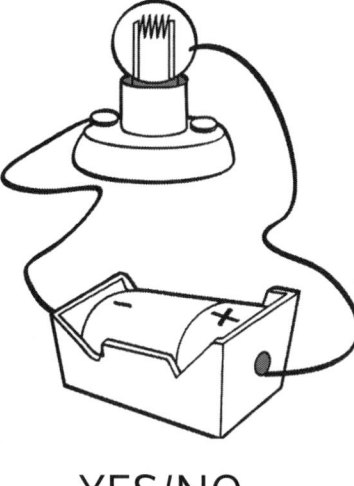

YES/NO

D

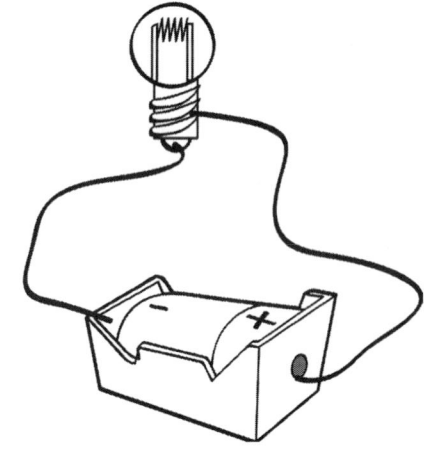

YES/NO

Make the circuits to find out.

Cambridge Primary Science 2

Make a bulb light up

Name: _____ Date: _____

Make circuits you have used. Cut and stick the bulbs and cells. Then draw the wires.

_____	_____
_____	_____

This circuit	did	did not	work.
The bulb	lit up.	did not	light up.

✂ -

Worksheet 5.3d

My circuits

Name: _____ Date: _____

Draw the circuits you have used. Write what happened.

_____ _____	_____ _____
_____ _____	_____ _____

Try to draw a circuit that uses two bulbs.

Cambridge Primary Science 2

© Cambridge University Press 2014

Worksheet 5.4a

Using motors and buzzers

Name: _____ Date: _____

Make circuits you have used. Cut and stick the cells, motor and buzzer. Then draw the wires. Write what happened in each circuit. Use the sentences below.

_____

_____

| The motor | turned. | did not | turn. |
| The buzzer | made | no sound. | a sound. |

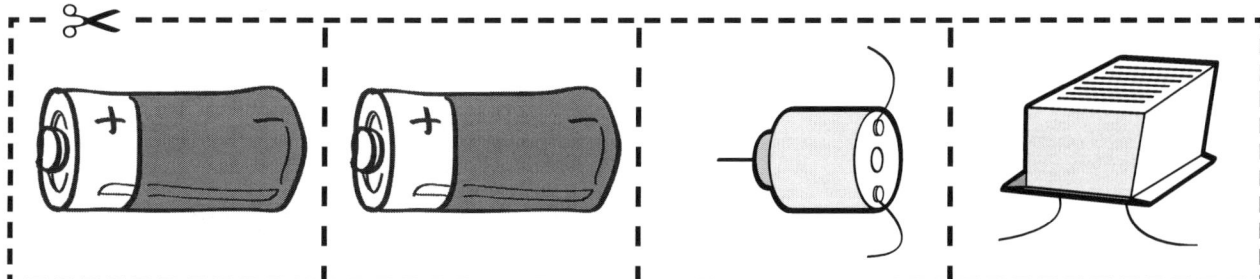

Worksheet 5.4b

Using motors and buzzers

Name: _____ Date: _____

Draw the circuits you have used. Write what happened in each circuit.

_____

_____

_____

_____

Cambridge Primary Science 2

Worksheet 5.5

Switch it on, switch it off

Name: _____ Date: _____

Make two circuits with a switch.

Cut and stick the switch, cells and the bulb, motor or buzzer.

Then draw the wires.

Write what happened in each circuit. Use the sentences below.

_____

_____

The switch		**was**	**on.**	**off.**
The bulb	**lit up.**	**did not**	**light up.**	
The motor	**turned.**	**did not**	**turn.**	
The buzzer	**buzzer.**	**did not**	**buzz.**	

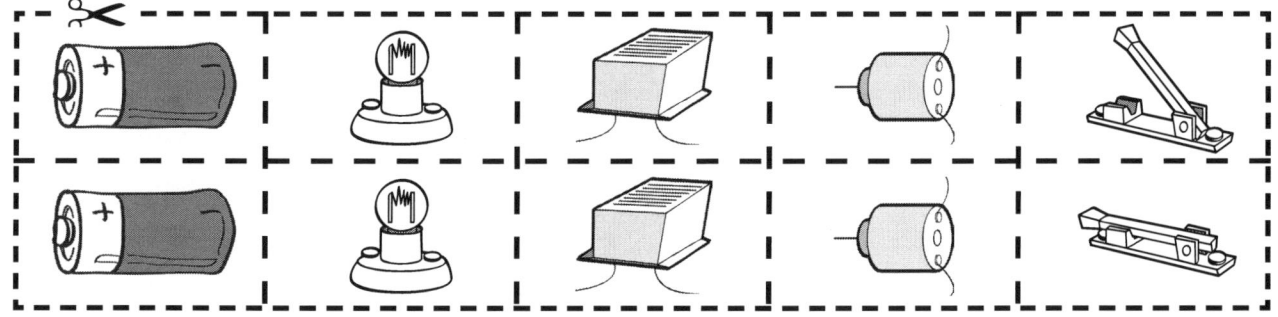

Unit 6

Teaching ideas

Background knowledge

At the time of the Polish astronomer Nicolaus Copernicus, the Earth was widely believed to be at the centre of the Universe. Copernicus challenged this 'geocentric' view with the idea of a 'heliocentric' model with the Sun at the centre. The Catholic Church disliked this theory. So, sixty years later, Galileo Galilei was put under house arrest by the Pope for strongly supporting the heliocentric model.

Today we know that the Sun is not at the centre of the Universe. But it is at the centre of our solar system. The planets of Mercury, Venus, Earth, Mars, Jupiter, Saturn, Uranus and Neptune all orbit the Sun.

Watching from Earth, we see the Sun move across the sky. At night, the stars and Moon follow similar paths. As a result, many learners will think that the Sun and stars orbit the Earth. It looks like this because the Earth spins on its axis; rotating once every twenty-four hours to give us night and day. When you spin around, it can seem as though it is everything around you that is spinning, even when you can feel the spinning. As we cannot feel the spinning of the Earth, it is easy to see why the 'geocentric' view was believed so strongly. Even today, many adults are unsure of the motions of the Sun, Earth and Moon.

Everywhere on Earth, the Sun rises in the east and sets in the west. This is because the Earth spins in an anticlockwise direction. On the Equator, and between the Tropic of Cancer in the Northern Hemisphere and the Tropic of Capricorn in the Southern Hemisphere, the Sun climbs very high in the sky. At midday it is often overhead, or almost overhead. From the rest of the Northern Hemisphere the Sun always looks lower in the sky, even at midday. It moves across the southern half of the sky and is due south at its highest point. From the rest of the Southern Hemisphere the Sun is again low in the sky and its path is across the northern half of the sky. It is due north at its highest point.

The Earth spins on its axis and the axis is tilted. This tilt results in the changing seasons and changes in the number of hours of daylight different parts of the Earth receive at different times of the year. As Earth makes its yearly orbit around the Sun, the direction of the tilt stays the same. So, in July the Northern Hemisphere is tilted towards the Sun and the Southern Hemisphere tilted away. In January, the opposite happens, the Northern Hemisphere tilts away from the Sun and the Southern Hemisphere tilts towards it. As a result, the hours of daylight during the summer months are longer than during the winter months.

The cooler average temperatures in winter are caused by light from the Sun being more spread out as it falls upon a more tilted surface. Because the light energy from the Sun is more spread out, it warms the surface of the Earth much less.

The Moon orbits the Earth and takes about 28 days for one orbit. As a result, the Moon can rise or set at any time of the day or night. For example, it can rise in the day and set after dark. Or, it can rise late in the night and be seen in the sky during the day. However, the Moon is not a source of light, it simply reflects light from the Sun towards Earth. Because of this it is much less bright than the Sun and can be hard to see during daylight. The Moon is far easier to see at night. This leads to two common misconceptions: that the Sun turns into the Moon at night and that the Sun is up in the day and the Moon is up at night.

In this unit there are many different words that could be used that have meanings similar to the word 'round'. For example turn, sphere, circle, spin, rotate, orbit and around. Choose the words you use with care and make sure that learners can check the different meanings by displaying the relevant vocabulary in the classroom.

Learners should be warned never to look directly at bright light sources, especially the Sun, as this can damage the eyes. Explain to learners how sunlight can cause sunburn, which can be painful and can cause skin cancer. Talk with learners about how to avoid sunburn by covering up bare skin and using sunscreen to give protection.

Unit overview

Topic	Number of lessons	Outline of lesson content	Resources in Learner's Book	Resources in Activity Book	Resources in Teacher's Resource
6.1 Day and night	1–2	Learners model how the rotation of the Earth leads to day and night using balls and torches.	Activity 6.1 Day and night SE Su Ex	Exercise 6.1 SE Su	Worksheet 6.1a SE L Ex Worksheet 6.1b SE Su Resource sheet 6.1 L Su
6.2 Does the Sun move?	1–2	Learners observe the position of the Sun in the sky at different times of the day.	Activity 6.2 Does the Sun move? SE Su Ex	Exercise 6.2 SE L	Worksheet 6.2a SE Worksheet 6.2b SE Su Resource sheet 6.2
6.3 Changing shadows	2–3	Learners observe and measure how shadows move due to Earth's rotation.	Activity 6.3a Do shadows move? SE Activity 6.3b Shadow length SE Ex	Exercise 6.3 SE Ex	Worksheet 6.3 SE
6.4 Check your progress			Questions 1 SE , 2, SE 3 SE		

Ex Extension   L Language   SE Enquiry   Su Support

Resource list

- toy people
- globes or footballs
- sticky tack
- light sources, such as torches
- hula hoops
- string (optional)
- a clock
- compasses
- card
- chalk
- cameras (optional)
- a pole (or a tree)
- pencils (two per pair or group)
- same-size plastic bricks, counters or coins
- large paper (one piece per pair or group)
- rulers
- larger objects as a non-standard measure, such as large counters, empty match boxes, identical unused erasers, playing cards

Topic 6.1 Day and night

In this topic, learners explore how day and night is caused by the rotation of the Earth.

Learning objectives

- Model how the spin of the Earth leads to day and night, e.g. with different-sized balls and a torch.
- Identify simple patterns and associations.

Curriculum links

- This unit has clear links to Unit 4 on shadows. In this topic, you could make it clear that 'night' is in fact the Earth's shadow as it blocks the light from the Sun.
- There are links to geography in this unit if you discuss which parts of the Earth are experiencing day or night when you look at pictures of the Earth.
- This topic links to physical education work in dance. Many of the activities involve movement, and a group dance could be developed.
- This topic could be linked to language work using the stories suggested.

Ideas for the lesson

- Find out what learners already know about the Earth and the Sun in space by reading a book and then asking them to talk about what they know. Any book about space will do but these are particularly good for young learners: *Is a Blue Whale the Biggest Thing There Is?* by Robert E. Wells; *There's No Place Like Space!* by Dr Seuss; or *Papa, Please Get the Moon for Me* by Eric Carle. Ask learners specifically about the shape of the Earth. Can learners say that it is round, like a ball? Ask them to explain how they know. They might say that they have seen pictures or that you can go all the way around the Earth. Show learners a picture of the Earth from space that shows it is a sphere. You could use the picture in the Learner's Book on page 60 for this. Picture 6.1 on the CD-ROM shows the same diagram, but with different parts of the Earth facing the Sun. You can use this to introduce the idea that the Earth turns, and this causes day and night.

- Activity 6.1 asks learners to model day and night using a ball and a torch. (See *Notes on practical activities* section.)

- Ask learners whether they have visited, or have relatives in, different countries around the world. Explain that when some countries have day, others have night. Show learners a globe with two toy figures, one on each side, and demonstrate that when one is in day the other is in night.

- Ask three learners to stand inside a hula hoop facing out with the hoop at their waists. Choose a fourth learner to shine a torch at the others. The learner with the torch is stationary and the learners in the hoop rotate. As the hoop rotates, the learners inside can mime what they would be doing at that time of day. On the side away from the light they can be asleep, as they come into the light they can wake up and stretch or clean their teeth. They can then eat some food and get ready for bed as they move away from the light again. Learners can work in groups of four to practise and perform this demonstration.

- The activity above can work with larger groups standing inside a loop of string or simply linking arms. Other learners can stand still around the outside of the rotating 'Earth' group holding time cards, yellow for day and blue for night.

- Worksheet 6.1a asks learners to identify simple patterns and associations by drawing what they are doing when the Earth is in different parts of its rotation. Worksheet 6.1b is similar, but is designed for use by higher achieving learners. It asks learners to describe the difference between night and day and to write what they do at different times.

- Show learners images from web cameras around the world. Choose two on opposite sides of the globe to demonstrate that night and day can happen at the same time but in different places. Show learners the time on each web cam and explain that they are all 'now' but the times are different in different parts of the world. There are some web cam links in the *Internet and ICT* section below.

- Activity Book Exercise 6.1 reinforces the learning in this topic. It asks learners to match activities to day or night regions of the Earth.

- Resource sheet 6.1 gives some vocabulary for this unit. Use it to support lower achieving learners, or use the cards as part of a wall display on this unit.

Notes on practical activities

Activity 6.1 Day and night

Each pair or group will need:
- a toy person
- a globe or football
- sticky tack
- a light source, such as a torch

If possible, darken the classroom by closing the blinds or putting dark paper over the windows.

Read Activity 6.1 in the Learner's Book and explain to learners how to model night and day for themselves using the equipment provided. To encourage learners to identify simple patterns and associations, talk with them about what the toy person might be doing when they are in the darker, night half of the Earth and what they might be doing in the lighter, day half. One pair could be asked to demonstrate while the others chant 'day' or 'night' as the 'Earth' rotates.

Internet and ICT

- Show learners the video of Eric Carle's story, *Papa, Please Get the Moon for Me*. It can be found at these websites: www.frequency.com/video/papa-please-get-moon-for-me/75456730 ; www.popscreen.com/v/5XLjG/Papa-please-get-the-moon-for-me ; vidaru.com/papa-please-get-the-moon-for-me/49540324.

- The following websites are webcam internet links:
  Hong Kong: www.weather.gov.hk/wxinfo/ts/webcam/CP1_photo_e.htm
  New York: www.earthcam.com/usa/newyork/timessquare/?cam=tsstreet;
  Sydney Harbour: www.earthcam.com/world/australia/sydney/;
  Abbey Road, London: www.abbeyroad.com/Crossing.

- There are a selection of webcams to choose from here: search.earthcam.com/network/.

- Show learners this short video of day and night on Earth as seen from the International Space Station: www.openculture.com/2010/09/a_day_on_earth_as_seen_from_space.html.

- The following link shows a very clear animation of how night and day happens – the text is for older learners but the images are useful for Stage 2: www.childrensuniversity.manchester.ac.uk/interactives/science/earthandbeyond/dayandnight/.

Assessment

- Using a torch and a toy person on a globe, ask learners to mime what the person might be doing as the globe rotates. Choose learners to explain what they are miming and challenge them to say why. Responses might include 'I am sleeping because it is night.'

Differentiation

- Support lower achieving learners in this unit by stopping the activities frequently. Then explain to learners, or ask learners to explain to you, what they are doing and why.

- Talk with higher achieving learners about how long the Earth takes to spin – 24 hours. Worksheet 6.1b can be used to support higher achieving learners.

Common misunderstandings and misconceptions

- Many learners will think that the Sun is in the sky in the day and the Moon is in the sky at night. Some may think that the Sun turns into the Moon at night. Show these learners pictures of the Moon in the sky in the day time. Talk with them about how it can be hard to see the Moon in the day because the Sun is so bright.

Homework ideas

- Activity Book Exercise 6.1 can be completed at home.
- Worksheets 6.1a and 6.1b are suitable homework activities.

Answers to Activity Book exercise

Exercise 6.1

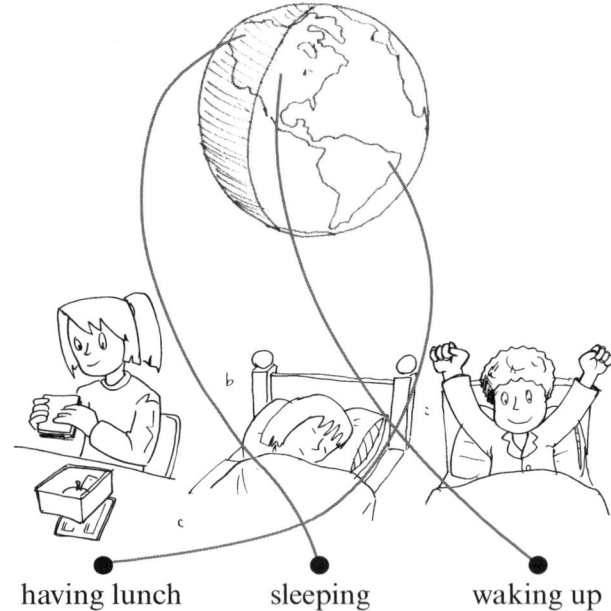

having lunch   sleeping   waking up

Answers to Worksheets

Worksheet 6.1a

Learners colour in each Sun and Earth and shade each Earth. The shading of each Earth should correctly illustrate the side of the Earth facing away from the Sun (in the dark), and the side of the Earth facing the Sun (in the light).

Learners draw what they do in the night and in the day. Accept any sensible drawings.

Worksheet 6.1b

Learners colour in each Sun and Earth and shade each Earth. The shading of each Earth should correctly illustrate the side of the Earth

facing away from the Sun (in the dark), and the side of the Earth facing the Sun (in the light).

In the **night**, where I live has **turned away** from the Sun. It is dark.

In the **day**, where I live has turned **towards** the Sun. It is **light**.

Learners also complete sentences to say what they like doing in the night and day. Accept any sensible sentences.

Topic 6.2 Does the Sun move?

In this topic, learners explore how the Sun *appears* to move during the day. (The next topic explores how shadows change as the Sun moves.)

Learning objectives

- Explore how the Sun appears to move during the day.
- Collect evidence by making observations when trying to answer a science question.
- Use first-hand experience.
- Make suggestions for collecting evidence.
- Talk about risks and how to avoid danger.
- Make and record observations.
- Take simple measurements.
- Use a variety of ways to tell others what happened.
- Identify simple patterns and associations.
- Review and explain what happened.

Curriculum links

- This topic has strong links with time and with position and movement in maths.

Ideas for the lesson

- Talk with learners about the picture on page 62 of the Learner's Book. Ask learners whether they agree with any of the statements. Ask them to say what they think. Some learners may give answers relating to movement of burning gases on the surface of the Sun. Make sure that these learners know that the question is asking whether the Sun moves from one place to another.
- Help learners to complete Activity 6.2 to gain first-hand experience of observing the apparent movement of the Sun. (See *Notes on practical activities* section.) Worksheet 6.2a supports this activity.

- **Note:** the picture on page 63 of the Learner's Book shows the Sun's apparent movement as seen looking south from the Northern Hemisphere. From the Southern Hemisphere, you would have to face north to see the Sun; it would be seen to move from right to left. Picture 6.2 on the CD-ROM is the mirror image of the artwork from the Learner's Book; you might prefer to use this if you are in the Southern Hemisphere, as it will be more relevant to your location. If you are near the equator, the Sun will appear to move overhead.

- Show learners a compass and teach them the names of the four main directions. Help learners use a compass to work out that the Sun rises in the east and sets in the west. **Note:** this may be the first time learners have been shown the points of the compass. The topic is not introduced in maths until Stage 3.

- Learners can use a compass card and themselves to model the Sun rising in the east and setting in the west. Give each learner a compass drawn on card – you could use Resource sheet 6.2. Ask the learners to stand holding the compass in front of them. Ask learners to pretend that their own head is the Earth and to turn their compass so that north is pointing upwards because the top of their head is the North Pole. Have a large picture of the Sun on one wall of the classroom and ask learners to turn so that east on their compass points towards the Sun. Then ask learners to turn towards the Sun – they should spin slowly like the Earth so that the Sun seems to move towards the west. They should complete half a turn. If they keep spinning the Sun goes down. They will not be able to see the Sun again until they have done another half turn and it rises again in the east.

- You could complete the activity above without using compass cards as a simpler demonstration of why the Sun appears to move across the sky.

- Learners can complete Worksheet 6.2b. This asks learners to make comparisons and simple associations by drawing what they do when it gets dark at night and when it gets light in the morning.

- In Activity Book Exercise 6.2, learners draw how the Sun appears to move across the sky during the day. They also draw an arrow to show how the Earth spins on its axis.

- Plan a class performance to tell others what happens. Learners can work as a class to demonstrate how the Sun looks as if it is moving across the sky from east to west, starting low at sunrise in the morning, rising until midday then getting lower again until sunset in the evening. Learners could also demonstrate the different times on the planet using the activities from Topic 6.1. These demonstrations could be set to music or performed as a dance.

Notes on practical activities

Activity 6.2 Does the Sun move?

Each pair or group will need:
- a sunny day
- a clock

Ask learners to make suggestions for collecting evidence about whether the Sun moves. Learners might suggest going outside to look at the Sun. Explain to learners that if the Sun moves very slowly they might not notice its movement. Ask them to think about how we see other very slow changes, such as plants growing. Help learners plan to go outside at different times in the day to look at the position of the Sun. Ask them to suggest what they could observe and what they could record. You could give learners a picture of the outside area so they can draw the Sun each time in relation to buildings or trees. Learners could also take simple measurements by recording the time when they observe the position of the Sun.

Before observing the position of the Sun, talk with learners about not looking directly at it. Talk about the risks and how to avoid danger.

Learners should be warned never to look directly at bright light sources, especially the Sun, as this can damage their eyes.

Take learners outside to identify simple patterns by drawing the position of the Sun at least three times in the day. Going near the start, middle and end of the school day will show the clearest differences. Learners can use Worksheet 6.2a to record their comparisons. You may wish to add some features of your outside area to the picture on the sheet to help learners position their drawings of the Sun on the picture.

Talk with learners about what they have observed. The Sun does move across the sky. Explain that this happens because the Earth is spinning – it is not the Sun moving. Ask learners if they have ever been on a roundabout. Ask learners to explain to others what you see on a roundabout when it is spinning or when you spin around while standing up. It looks like the world is spinning around you. But actually it is you moving not the world. Explain that this is what is happening with the Sun. The Earth is spinning so it looks as if the Sun is moving. If possible, use a rotating chair to give learners the opportunity to experience spinning.

 Do not let learners spin the chair too fast as they might get dizzy or fall off.
Safety

Internet and ICT

- Use an online planetarium, or the free Stellarium software, to show learners how the Moon and stars also seem to move across the sky with the Sun. These both have a feature that allows viewing of the sky without an atmosphere. This makes the stars visible with the Sun during daytime. See these website links: neave.com/planetarium/ and www.stellarium.org/.

Assessment

- Ask learners to work in small groups to prepare an explanation for others on how the Sun seems to move in the sky. Learners could use a cardboard Sun. Talk with learners about their explanations and ask each group to present their explanation to the class.

Differentiation

- Support lower achieving learners in Activity 6.2 by reminding them how to read the time to the nearest hour before starting this investigation. These learners could record the position of the Sun on the hour. All the times could be set at the beginning of the activity and learners could draw the hands on all of the clock faces at the beginning of the day. Some learners may need an adult to draw the times on the clock faces for them.

- In Activity 6.2, challenge higher achieving learners by showing them how to use a compass and asking them to use it to record the position of the Sun. These learners could be taught about the four main compass directions: north, east, south and west. The direction of the Sun could be recorded as 'close to east' or 'towards the west'.

Common misunderstandings and misconceptions

- Many learners will think that the Earth remains still and the Sun moves. The activities in this unit will begin to challenge this misconception. But learners will need many repetitions or reminders of these experiences to secure their understanding.

- Some learners may know that the Sun is made of burning gases and the surface is very active. Make sure that these learners know that the question 'Does the Sun move?' is not asking about whether there is movement on the Sun's surface.

Homework ideas

- Ask learners to watch to see where the Sun comes up and/or goes down near their home. Note: this may only be possible at certain times of the year depending on the times of sunset, sunrise and learners' bedtimes.

- Activity Book Exercise 6.2 can be completed at home.

- Worksheet 6.2b is a suitable homework activity.

Answers to Activity Book exercise

Exercise 6.2

Answers to Worksheets

Worksheet 6.2a

The times recorded by learners, and their drawings of the position of the Sun, will depend on the times of the day that learners went outside to observe the Sun. Accept any sensible time recordings and Sun drawings. Some learners may have observed that the Sun is highest near midday and lower earlier and later.

Worksheet 6.2b

Learners draw what they do when the Sun comes up and when it goes down. Accept any sensible drawings.

Topic 6.3 Changing shadows

In this topic, learners continue to learn about the consequences of the Earth's rotation (the apparent movement of the Sun) by considering how shadows change.

Learning objectives

- Explore how shadows change.
- Collect evidence by making observations when trying to answer a science question.
- Use first-hand experience.
- Ask questions and suggest ways to answer them.
- Predict what will happen before deciding what to do.
- Recognise that a test or comparison may be unfair.
- Make suggestions for collecting evidence.
- Talk about risks and how to avoid danger.
- Make and record observations.
- Take simple measurements.
- Identify simple patterns and associations.

Curriculum links

- This topic links with Unit 4 on shadows.
- There are links with maths as learners practise measuring.

Ideas for the lesson

- Remind learners of the work done in Topic 4.3 Making shadows and Topic 4.4 Shadow shapes. Ask learners to say what they remember about going outside to look at shadows.
- Activity 6.3a asks learners to try to answer the question 'Do shadows move?' by drawing around their shadows outside and observing how they change throughout the day. (See *Notes on practical activities* section.)
- Look at the picture of the sundial in the Learner's Book and ask if any learners can explain what it does. Discuss how a sundial works. Then make a sundial with learners by marking the position of the shadow of a pole or a tree at each hour of the day. You could use chalk or even paint for a more permanent sundial. Teach learners how to use the sundial to tell the time on the hour and half past the hour (when the shadow is halfway between two hours). **Note:** in countries that change their clocks for daylight saving, the sundial will need renumbering when the clocks are changed.
- Activity 6.3b asks learners to measure the shadow of a pencil throughout the day to see how the length changes. (See *Notes on practical activities* section.) Worksheet 6.3 supports this activity.
- Activity Book Exercise 6.3 asks learners to measure the length of shadows using plastic bricks, coins or counters. Whichever object is used, each one must be of the same size to make sure the comparison is fair. Higher achieving learners could measure with a ruler to the nearest centimetre.
- Picture 6.3 on the CD-ROM consolidates the learning for the lesson. It shows the Sun and shadows at three different times of day. Ask learners to describe and explain the shadows in the pictures. You can also show them the pictures of shadows in the Learner's book.

Notes on practical activities

Activity 6.3a Do shadows move?

Each pair or group will need:
- chalk
- a sunny day

This activity needs to be completed on a sunny day. Learners use first-hand experience and will need to work in pairs.

To introduce Activity 6.3a, ask learners to think back to the previous topic where they learnt that the Sun seems to move across the sky. Ask learners to predict what this might do to their shadows. Encourage learners to ask questions about how their shadows might change. Some learners might ask whether their shadows will get bigger or smaller or whether they will move. Others may be able to be more specific, asking whether their shadows will get longer, shorter, wider, or narrower or whether they might turn or move along. Ask learners to tell their questions to the class and to predict the answer. Ask other learners whether they agree or disagree with the predictions. Some learners may be able to justify their answers.

Encourage learners to make suggestions about how they can answer their questions. Help them to plan to go outside several times in the day and to draw around their shadows with chalk each time. Ask learners to think about why it is important to stand in the same place each time. Encourage learners to recognise that the test would be unfair if they did not do this.

Ask learners to observe the position of each shadow carefully. Can they see how the shadow position has changed each time they go outside? Learners could use a camera to photograph the chalk marks and their later shadows. You could look at these photographs with learners and discuss them back in class.

Each time you go outside, ask learners to point at their shadow with one hand and at the Sun with the other. Talk with learners about how these two directions are always opposite. This will help learners to identify the association.

Before observing the position of the Sun, talk with learners about not looking directly at it. Talk about the risks and how to avoid danger.

 Learners should be warned never to look directly at bright light sources, especially the Sun, as this can damage their eyes.

Activity 6.3b Shadow length

Each pair or group will need:
- two pencils
- sticky tack
- a clock
- same-size plastic bricks, counters or coins
- a large piece of paper
- a sunny day

Ask learners to suggest what evidence they can collect to answer the question 'Does the length of a shadow change?' Some learners might suggest marking the shadow at different times so any changes in length can be observed. Others might suggest that they can measure the length either with non-standard units or in centimetres.

Read Activity 6.3b in the Learner's Book. Then show learners how to take a simple measurement of the length of the shadow by making a line of same-sized bricks, counters or coins and counting the number used. Higher achieving learners could use rulers.

Ask learners to check the clock and to mark and measure the length of the shadows every hour throughout the day. Learners can record the time of each measurement and the shadow length in a table. Worksheet 6.3 could be used.

Talk with learners about not looking directly at the Sun. Talk about the risks and how to avoid danger.

 Learners should be warned never to look directly at bright light sources, especially the Sun, as this can damage their eyes.

Talk with learners about how to keep the test fair. Ask them to think about what they need to keep the same. Learners will need to use the same pencil each time and put it in the same position. They could mark with chalk the position of the paper, in case it moves between measurements.

After the activity, help learners to identify the pattern in the results. The shadow will get shorter towards the middle of the day and then get longer again. Learners could make a tower out of bricks for each measurement to help them see the pattern.

Internet and ICT

- Learners can use these online simulations to see how shadows change throughout the day: www.childrensuniversity.manchester.ac.uk/interactives/science/earthandbeyond/shadows/ and www.bbc.co.uk/schools/scienceclips/ages/7_8/light_shadows.shtml – choose the 'Outside' option.

Assessment

- Towards the end of the Activity 6.3b, ask groups of learners to swap over and check each other's measurements using the bricks, counters or coins. Then ask the groups to compare their measurements. **Note:** the shape of the sticky tack base holding up the pencil may affect the accuracy of the measurements. Encourage learners to measure to the pencil rather than the base.

- Ask learners to investigate the length of the shadow of a toy person using a torch at different heights. Learners could put the toy person on a sheet of paper and shade in some of the different shadows they make. Ask some learners to show their drawn shadows to others and to explain how they made the shadows that are very long or very short.

Differentiation

- To keep the numbers small, lower achieving learners may need to use larger objects as a non-standard measure in Activity 6.3b. Larger counters, empty match boxes, identical unused erasers or even playing cards could be used.

- Higher achieving learners could measure the length of the shadow of their pencil in Activity 6.3b to the nearest centimetre. An extra challenge could be to record the compass direction of the shadow each time.

Common misunderstandings and misconceptions

- In Activity 6.3b, learners will see the length of the shadow getting shorter in the morning. But, many will think that it will continue to shorten throughout the afternoon. Ask these learners to think about the previous topic and the position of the Sun in the sky in the morning and evening. Also remind them of Activity 6.3a when they pointed at their shadow with one hand and the Sun with the other. Completing Activity 6.3b will help them to associate the position of the Sun with the length of the shadow.

Homework ideas

- If learners have access to cameras at home, ask them to photograph long shadows of themselves late in the evening and bring the pictures into school to show and discuss with others. Make it clear that learners will need to ask for permission and help from adults at home to use digital cameras.

- Activity Book Exercise 6.3 could be completed at home.

Answers to Activity Book exercise

Exercise 6.3

The measured lengths of the shadows will depend on the size of bricks, counters or coins used. Accept any sensible answers.

The time of the shortest shadow is 12.00 p.m.

Answers to Worksheet

Worksheet 6.3

The times recorded will depend on the times of day that learners went outside. The measured lengths of the shadows will depend on the size of bricks, counters or coins used. Accept any sensible answers.

The shadow will be longest at the earliest or latest time of day recorded.

The shadow will be shortest at the time of day closest to 12.00 p.m.

Topic 6.4 Check your progress

Learning objectives

- Review the learning for this unit.

Ideas for the lesson

- Learners can be asked to answer the questions on the 'Check your progress' pages of the Learner's Book. These questions cover topics from the whole unit. Some answers are ambiguous, which will lead to discussion that will help to assess learners' understanding of this unit.

Answers to Learner's Book questions

1   Manu is in day because he is on the side of the Earth that is lit up by the Sun.
    Kun is in night because she is on the side of the Earth that is not lit up by the Sun.

2   Picture A is correct. The Earth spins and it looks like the Sun is moving.
    Picture B is incorrect. The Sun does not go round the Earth but it looks like it does from Earth because the Earth spins.

3   a   In picture A, the people have short shadows so the Sun is high in the sky.
        In picture B, the people have long shadows so the Sun is low in the sky.
    b   Picture A must have been taken near the middle of the day. It could be around 11 a.m., midday or 1 p.m.
        Picture B could have been taken early in the morning or late in the evening.

Resource sheet 6.1

Vocabulary Cards

spin	
day	
night	
Sun	
high	
low	
east	
west	
north	
south	

Compass cards

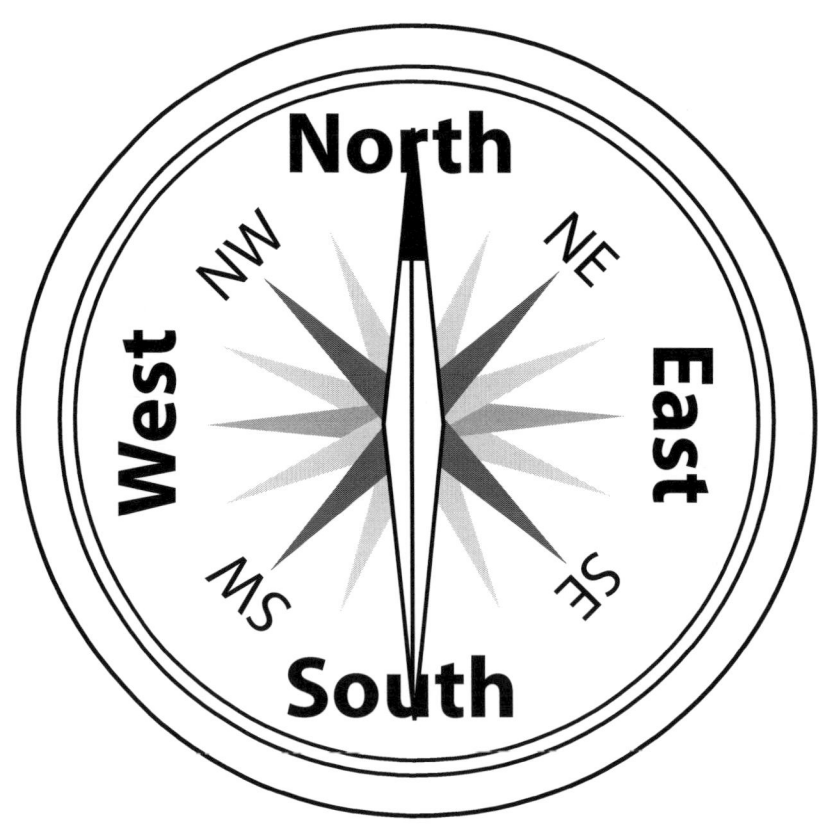

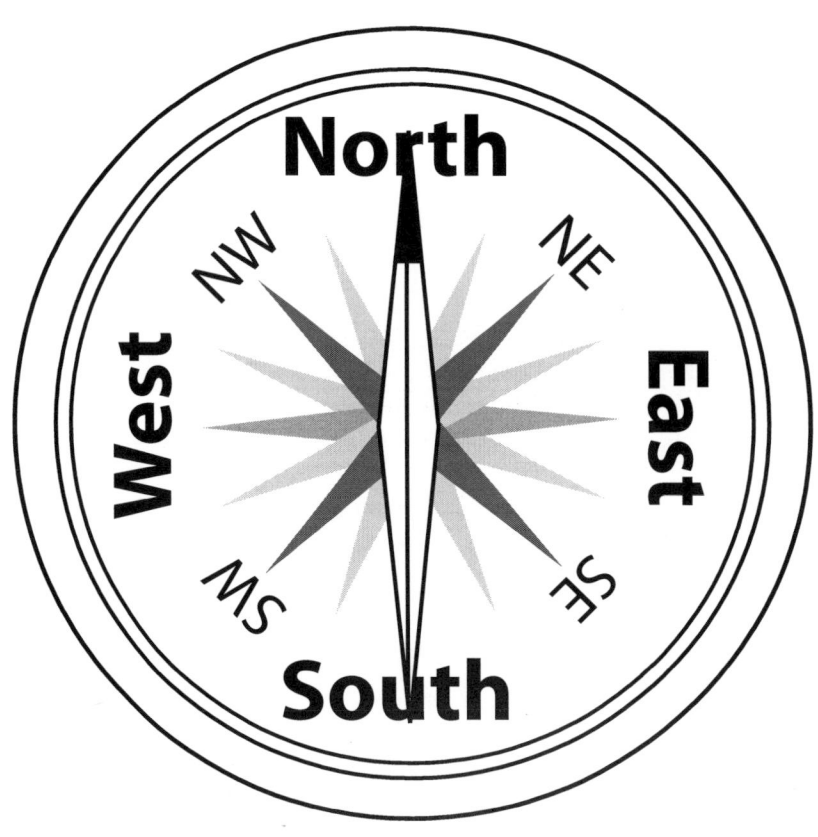

Cambridge Primary Science 2

Worksheet 6.1a

Day and night 1

Name: _____ Date: _____

Colour the Sun and Earth.

Shade the Earth to show night and day.

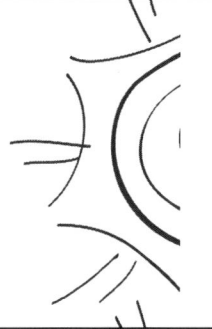

Night
Draw what
you do at
night.

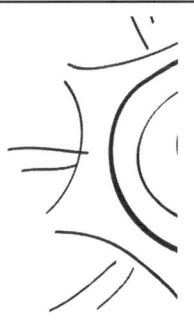

Day
Draw what
you do in
the day.

Worksheet 6.1b

Day and night 2

Name: _____ Date: _____

Colour the Sun and Earth.

Shade the Earth to show night and day.

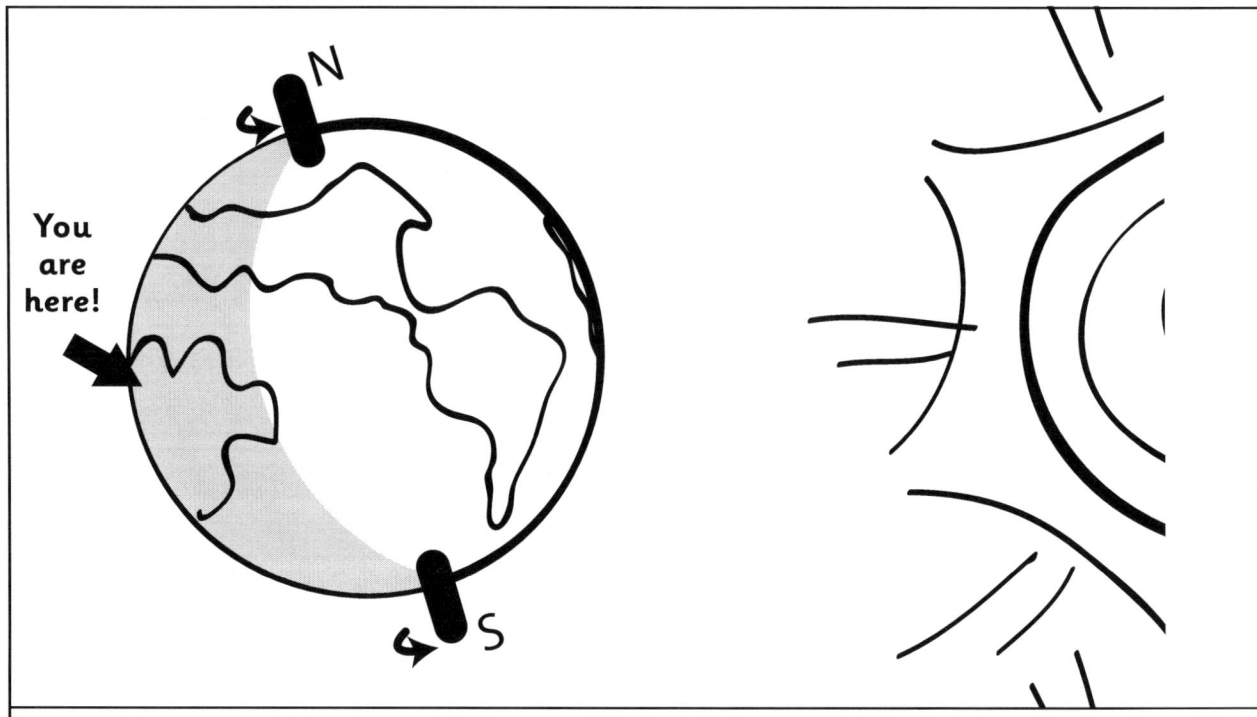

In the _____, where I live has turned _____
_____ the Sun. It is _____.

Use these words

away from   dark   night

Finish this sentence.
In the night, I like to

_____

Worksheet 6.1b

Colour the Sun and Earth.

Shade the Earth to show night and day.

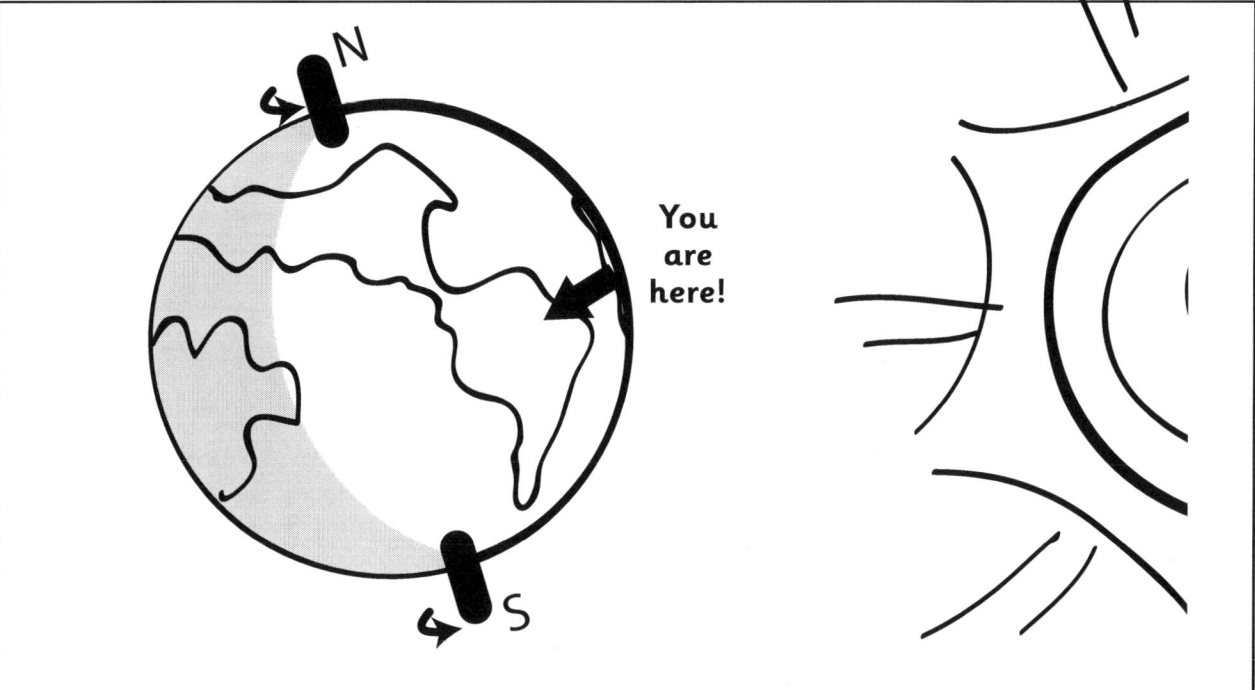

In the _____, where I live has turned _____
the Sun. It is _____.

Use these words

day	light	towards

Finish this sentence.
In the day, I like to

_____

Worksheet 6.2a

Does the Sun move?

Name: _____ Date: _____

Draw where the Sun is in the sky at different times.
Record the time.

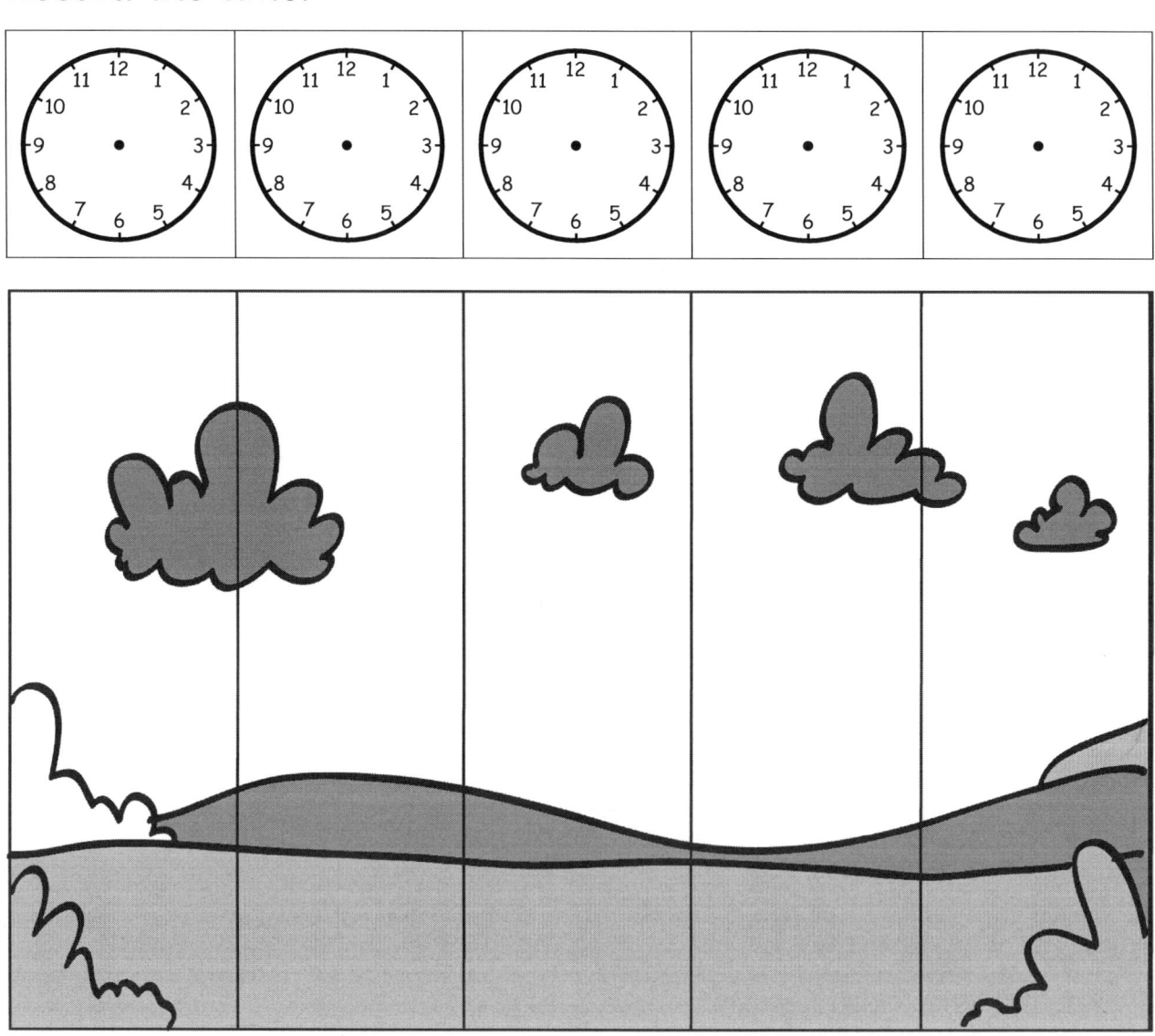

When is the Sun high? When is the Sun low?

Cambridge Primary Science 2

Worksheet 6.2b

What do you do at different times?

Name: _____ Date: _____

Draw what you do when the Sun comes up.

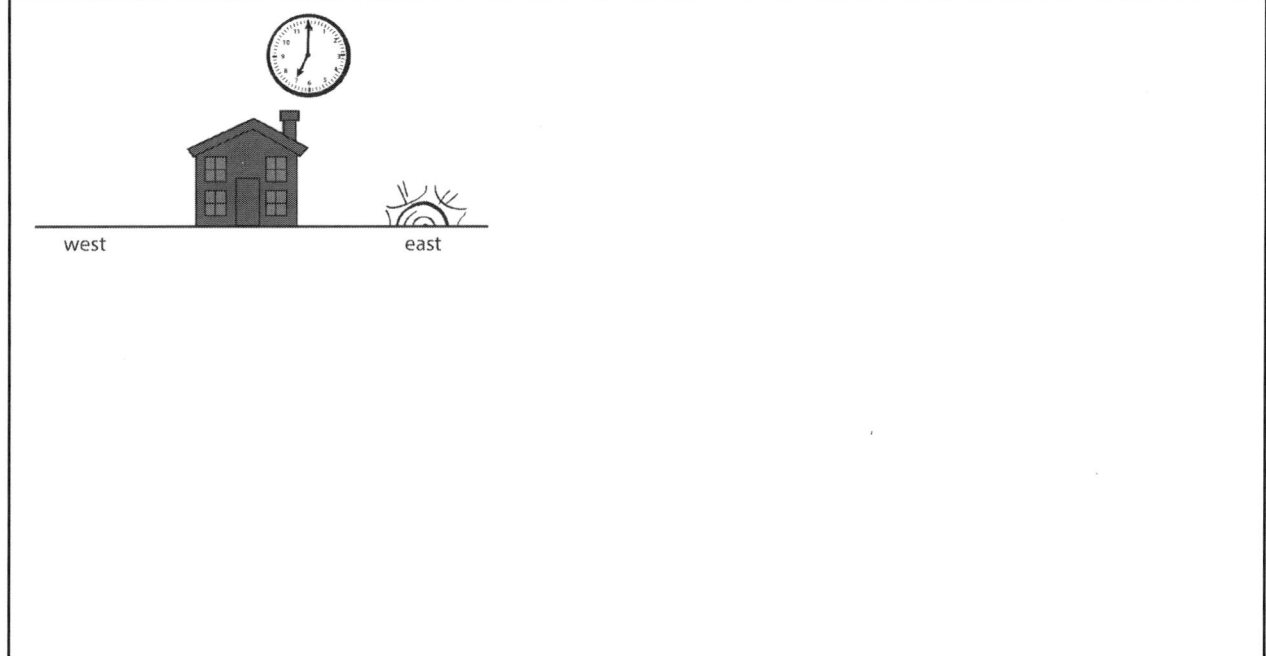

Draw what you do when the Sun goes down.

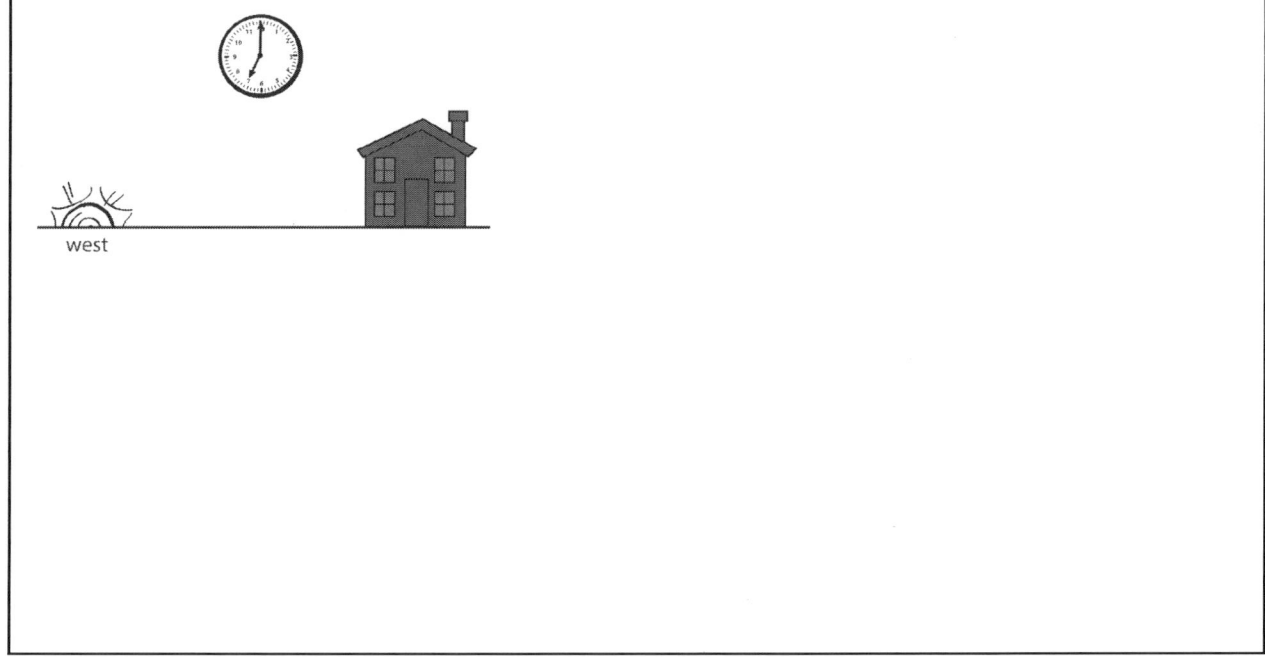

Worksheet 6.3

Measuring shadows

Name: _____ Date: _____

Measure the length of a shadow at different times in the day. You could use plastic bricks, counters or a ruler to measure the shadow.

Time	Length of shadow

When was the shadow longest? _____

When was it shortest? _____